# NEALE ANALYSIS
# OF READING ABILITY
## *REVISED BRITISH EDITION*

# NEALE ANALYSIS OF READING ABILITY
## *REVISED BRITISH EDITION*

# MANUAL

Marie D.Neale

*British adaptation and standardization by*
Una Christophers *and* Chris Whetton

NFER-NELSON

*Neale Analysis of Reading Ability – Revised* first published by the Australian Council for Educational Research, 1988.

This edition published by The NFER-NELSON Publishing Company Ltd, Darville House, 2 Oxford Road East, Windsor, Berkshire SL4 1DF by arrangement with the Australian Council for Educational Research Limited.

Printed in Great Britain
ISBN 0 7005 1225X
Code 2301 012
2(9.89)

# DEDICATION

To the memory of my Father,
and
to my Mother
whose wisdom has been an unfailing oasis.

# Contents

CHAPTER 1

## Introduction                                                         *1*

CHAPTER 2

## Description of the Neale Analysis of Reading Ability – Revised        *6*

CHAPTER 3

## Administering and Scoring the Standardized Tests                     *9*

CHAPTER 4

## Diagnostic Tutor Form                                                *23*

# List of Figures

# List of Tables

# Preface

Quality in education (the pursuit of excellence) and intervention to break the cycle of low self-esteem and learning failure are just two of the many constructs that characterize contemporary educational discourse. While debate can be assured on any one issue, the common denominator is a recognition that literacy, and more specifically the art of reading, is crucial to the cognitive development of the individual and to cementing the diverse networks of a modern society.

Schools have a primary responsibility for standards of instruction and they require reliable and valid measures of monitoring the success of their endeavours. The original Neale Analysis of Reading Ability broke new ground in the field of testing when it was first published in 1958, nearly thirty years ago. Since then, many features that were considered innovatory − for example, the testing of a child's accuracy in oral reading within a narrative context, the format of a picture story book with graded passages, the categorization of errors as a starting point for diagnostic and remedial work, and its style of structured interview for a sympathatice appraisal of the learner's aptitudes and limitations in language − have been accepted widely.

The Neale Analysis of Reading Ability − Revised builds upon these features with a concern that the individual's development and style of cognitive processing should be observed empathetically and as validly as possible. It affirms my original position that normative scores, while important for objective evidence of standards, are less relevant than diagnostic analyses for sensitive intervention and for orienting the learner to a fresh perspective of reading as a natural and pleasurable activity.

That reading is a means for acquiring information requires no emphasis, but what must be reiterated passionately is that the reading process itself is a means for the growth and well-being of individuals − cognitively, socially, and emotionally.

The Neale Analysis Reading Abiltiy − Revised rests on current community awareness of the need for teachers, psychologists, therapists, and parents to have common reference measures in order to conceptualize their standards and their accountability in the methods they employ for inducting the young into our conventions for depicting knowledge.

Those familiar with the Neale Analysis will recognize the theoretical constructs from child development that characterized the original work. Although there are significant changes in this publication, well-documented and proven features of the Analysis have been retained with fresh procedures of importance to modern testing and teaching. The trusting relationship that the Analysis sets up between the teacher and the student elicits the language of the individual for use in illuminating the role of reading and listening skills, the links between comprehension and syntax, and the significance of the rate of processing language in understanding and recall.

All parts of the work, the Reader, the Manual, and the Record Forms, have been revised in the light of data from clinical studies, research, and extensive field testing. While the validation studies have been carried out with the rigour usually accorded the construction of an intelligence test, considerable flexibility in style of assessment is promoted through the provision of alternative parallel forms of the Neale Analysis. Many professional workers will welcome the Diagnostic Tutor Form which, while tested and allocated to broad stage and grade bands, can be manipulated, modified, and used as both testing and teaching material before the child is tested formally on the revised standardized forms.

Another valuable addition to the expanded Manual is the inclusion of my formula for using the individual student's test data in a direct style of teaching to help the individual read for meaning, enjoy diverse ways of breaking the code, and find pleasure in the critical evaluation of text. Such an approach is seen as complementary to the teacher's own reading schemes, but it will also be a guide to the many therapists from different disciplines who now carry out testing and assist youth and adults to acquire competence and confidence in reading.

The original work took me almost four years, single-handed, to write the narratives, test them extensively against a wide range of reading materials, and standardize them into a battery of attainment and diagnostic tests presented as a story booklet and examiner's manual. This current revision has taken almost as long, and although there has been assistance in the data gathering and statistical analyses, I have again been responsible for writing original narratives and testing them in pilot and clinical studies. A survey of consumer opinion regarding the use of the Neale Analysis, suggested improvements, and the close monitoring of children's responses to the modified materials were time-consuming. The temptation to use multiple authors has been resisted in order to maintain the coherent internal structure of the items and to avoid the problems that arise from differences in writer's styles, or in their treatment of themes. They have resulted, however, in a sense of integrity in the items of 'standard' English text, which embody a central theme and a structured story line.

Over several decades, my use of the Neale Analysis, both as a diagnostic and attainment test even with children who exhibited developmental anomalies, has confirmed my optimism in the adaptability of the young when given the benefit of informed teaching and personal encouragement.

Moreover, in designing behavioural contexts and enrichment programs with teams of multi-disciplinary specialists to enhance the gifts of the very able child, who needs head room or specific assistance with aspects of literacy, I have had my faith reaffirmed in the creativity and dedication of teachers and therapists, particularly when diagnostic testing can pinpoint the special needs of the individual. I hope, therefore, that the Neale Analysis of Reading Ability − Revised, with its orientation to contemporary research in reading, and affirmation of the rights of individuals to knowledge through literacy, will serve as a useful tool for the many professionals who assist young people in acquiring communication skills.

Marie D. Neale
1987

# Acknowledgements

I wish to express my gratitude to a number of people. They range from those teachers and students in Victoria and South Australia who have helped in the data gathering, to the many schools and their pupils who took part, and to those who assisted in collating and marking thousands of records before any analysis could begin.

In particular, I wish to record my warmest appreciation to Dr Michael McKay for his cooperation and identification with every phase of this revision. His assistance in the standardization, from the pilot studies to the supervision of the testing in Victoria, to the statistical analyses of the data, to the final production, has been invaluable.

Finally, I owe my family an enormous debt for their loving support in the many vicissitudes I have endured in getting this revised work into published form to serve those who share my belief that teaching children is a privilege and a responsibility, as well as being an exciting enterprise.

Marie D. Neale 1987

The British Standardization of the Neale Analysis of Reading Ability – Revised could only have been undertaken with the enthusiastic support of the schools and teaching staff involved, in England and Wales. The National Foundation for Educational Research and the publishers, NFER-Nelson, wish to thank the many teachers and pupils who gave their time willingly to make this standardization possible.

Thanks and appreciation are due also to Mr Cres Fernandes, statistician at NFER, and to Mrs Barbara Bloomfield, Head of Field Research Services at NFER, for her organization of the data collection. We are also grateful to Mary Hargreaves, Mavis Froud and Pat Gibson at NFER for their help on this project.

Una Christophers and Chris Whetton 1989

# CHAPTER 1

# Introduction

## The Revision

Since the Neale Analysis of Reading Ability was first published in 1958, it has become one of the most widely used tests of reading in the United Kingdom, Australia and New Zealand. The range of its usefulness and versatility, from individual diagnostic work to large-scale research projects, is evident in the substantial body of research studies that have used the Neale Analysis to measure reading performance.

During recent years the need became apparent for a revision which would retain and enhance the valued features of the test, at the same time providing up-to-date norms, modernising a few of the passages and setting the whole in a context of current educational practice. The increasing use of the test as a diagnostic aid in schools highlighted the need to supply detailed suggestions on the interpretation of results and guidance on follow-up action. Steps were taken, therefore, in 1980, to review the test, which culminated in a revision and the Australian standardization in 1984, published by the Australian Council for Educational Research in 1988. A British Edition, reflecting the performance of children in England and Wales, was a natural follow-up and this work was conducted in 1988 by Una Christophers and Chris Whetton at the National Foundation for Educational Research.

## Background

At the time of the construction of the original Neale Analysis, reading assessments tended to mirror teaching methods and emphasized graded word lists (e.g. Vernon, 1938; Schonell, 1948), or the reading of isolated and unrelated sentences (e.g. Holborn Reading Scale) and single prose passages that covered too wide an age range for discriminative measures in accuracy and comprehension (e.g. Gates, 1947; Schonell, 1950). Alternatives in the form of silent reading tests presented considerable difficulties for differential diagnosis.

Three broad fields of psychology provided the theoretical framework for the development of the original Neale Analysis of Reading Ability – child development, social psychology, and perceptual psychology. The early work of Thurstone (1944) on perception, the experimental studies of Bruner and Postman (1949), and Solomon and Postman (1951) stimulated an awareness of the significance of hypothesis testing in the reading process. Bruner and Postman attributed an important role to perceptual expectancy in which individuals are predisposed by 'sets' that assist them in selecting, organizing, and transforming information obtained through the sensory channels. Stimulus information thus provides the individual with cues for forming, confirming, and denying hypotheses, and these hypotheses will depend upon the frequency of past confirmation.

The work of James and Eleanor Gibson in the 1950s (see, for example, Gibson & Gibson, 1955) took up the issue of perceptual learning in which the individual recognizes variations of physical stimuli not responded to previously. The Gibsons were to provide evidence that the learning of specific responses to objects and materials requires the child to be able to identify the differences between these and other objects; that is, he or she must be able to discriminate the specific qualities and dimensions that characterize an item. Nevertheless, while emphasizing the perceptual aspects of the reading process, they recognized that concepts from other theoretical positions (for example, the developmental basis for motor responses and a theory of cognitive development) must be incorporated into our understanding of the reading process.

In the field of reading, the work of pioneers such as Huey, Gray, Dearborn, Dolch, Durrell, Gates, Gilmore, and Schonell provided literary source material as well as models of test construction for the original Neale Analysis (Neale, 1958). In the intervening years the work of these theorists has been elaborated extensively and a wealth of other theory-based research in reading has been accumulated from the diverse fields of psycholinguistics, information processing, neurophysiology, clinical studies, and experimental studies of reading instruction as exemplified by the work of such authors as Boder (1973), Bradley & Bryant (1981 & 1983), Clark (1970), Clay (1979), Coltheart, Patterson & Marshall (1980), Downing & Leong (1982), Ellis & Miles (1981), Goodman (1968), Goodman & Burke (1972), Jorm (1983), Mitchell (1982), Neisser (1967), Pumfrey (1977), Satz (1976), Thomson (1984), Vernon (1977) among others.

The position adopted by Neale is that reading is part of the language system interacting with and serving the adaptive needs of the individual in conjunction with the physical, sensorimotor, and emotional systems. It is thus subject to the principles of child growth and development, its patterning influenced by the integrity of the central nervous system and both the broad and immediate social context.

There is now a substantial body of different kinds of studies that have used the Neale Analysis, for example:

- epidemiological studies (Rutter, Tizard & Whitmore, 1970);
- surveys of reading standards (e.g. the Bullock Report, Department of Education and Science 1975; Andrews & Elkins, 1971);
- differential diagnosis of reading performance (Yule, 1973; Yule, Lansdown, & Urbanowicz, 1982);
- experimental studies of different treatment or teaching methods (Downing, 1965; Riding & Pugh, 1977; Bradley & Bryant, 1981; le Coultre & Carroll, 1981; and Dyson & Swinson, 1982);
- clinical studies (Stores, 1978; Chadwick, Rutter, Thomson, & Shaffer, 1981; Rutter, Chadwick, Shaffer, & Brown, 1980; Stedman & Van Heyningen, 1982);
- studies of reading disability (Hornsby & Miles, 1980; Badcock & Lovegrove, 1981; Lovegrove, Martin, Bowling, Blackwood, Badcock, & Paxton, 1982; Johnston, Prior, & Hay, 1984; Hay, O'Brien, Johnston, & Prior, 1984);
- developmental studies of children's reading errors (Harding, Beech, & Sneddon, 1985);
- studies of informal reading analysis (Burke, 1977);
- academic studies by university students in higher degree work;
- extensive studies in schools using it as a measure of reading achievement (Goodacre, White, & Brennan, 1980);
- assessment in Braille of the reading skills of children with visual impairment (Lorimer, 1977);
- computer-guided educational diagnosis with a selected battery of reading tests (Colbourn & McLeod, 1983);

● as the model for designing other recent tests (Vincent & De la Mare, 1985).

This record appears to vindicate the exhaustive groundwork underlying Neale's construction of the original measure to accommodate a broad theoretical position with specific criteria for creating a multi-faceted appraisal of a child's reading behaviour. One can assess the strengths and weaknesses of the component skills of the reading process while not assuming that these components are sufficient in themselves to explain a child's total reading behaviour.

## Rationale

The following points, although not an elaborate theoretical treatment, may serve the test user in the interpretation of data derived from assessments using the Neale Analysis.

● In contrast to the immediacy of outcomes in experimental work, changes in child growth and development require time.
  − It is therefore necessary to be aware that complex interactions must be taken into account in any interpretation of such development, as it affects language, or changes in reading behaviour in response to teaching.

● Measurements of growth and development are typically expressed both in ages and stages. Age data represent the general, or 'average' trend for a particular aspect of behaviour observed from large numbers of children. However, it is important to recognize that considerable variations occur among individuals in attaining different stages of development.
  − Individual appraisal is important if valid information is to be obtained.

● Information processing is dependent upon the integrity of the individual's central nervous system − the integrity of the senses and motor coordination. Within the physical development of children, variations occur in the development of control over gross and fine motor movements and in the competence and speed of execution of those movements.
  − Clinical data and qualitative observations of the individual during testing may have considerable bearing on the planning of reading and associated language activities instigated as a consequence of testing.

● Language and communication skills serve functional and expressive purposes. They meet personal and social needs and are subject to elaboration through use, instruction, and social intercourse.
  − All stages of the teaching of reading should be seen in the larger context of literacy. The new Diagnostic Tutor Form allows this view to be adopted right from the initial testing.

● Social and emotional development, like language, also rests upon constitutional, temperamental, and experiential factors. Child rearing practices and socialization influence the pattern of social and emotional growth, but increasingly the interests, pursuits, and information processing styles of the individual play a significant role.
  − Idiosyncratic ways of symbolic processing, which can create difficulties for the school beginner in grappling with reading instruction, should be noted and taken into account for teaching.

● Adaptation and learning constitute a fourth system in child development, interweaving and spiralling with physical development, linguistic development, and social and emotional maturation. The constellation of adaptive responses through move-ment, exploration, investigation, and problem solving evolves into patterns of lan-guage and thought.

- Planning, logical sequences of thought, hypothesis testing, inferential thinking, which should all come to characterize the individual's style of learning, can be observed in testing and encouraged in the teaching of reading.

● For some individuals, originality, unconventional solutions to problems, and unusual juxtapositions of ideas do not fuse with conventional strategies of encoding.

- Systematic instruction in the structure of the language should also be com-plemented by provision of opportunities for individuals to express themselves in their own way, which allows them to develop their particular creativity.

● The foregoing processes are interwoven according to the individual's maturational tempo. Sometimes the child's language dominates the picture of growth, while at another phase the physical or emotional and social processes appear as the most significant aspect of development. It is accepted that there are some phases that are more sensitive to socializing influences or the deprivation of basic needs for activity, love and nurture, linguistic stimulation, achievement, and worthwhile purposes.

- Differences in maturational tempo are most evident in the school beginner. The 'appraisal and teaching cycle' in the early years of school should take account of an individual's rate of growth and the fulfilment of these basic needs.

● Each individual realizes his or her human potential only through acceptance and relationships with others, thereby acquiring the conventional communication skills and building upon personalized styles of perceiving the world.

- Auditory and visual signals are synthesized in language. In reading they must be synchronized speedily according to an arbitrary, given, conventional sequence, and must take account of varying styles of print. Rate of reading serves diagnostic purposes.

● The motor functions of the central nervous system for processing patterns of light and sound, and for selecting and discriminating between similar patterns of stimuli, are so personally organized that it is inevitable that there will be individual difficulties in response to classroom instruction in the processes of reading, writing, spelling, and language. The Neale Analysis focuses on the child as an individual whose growth, motor system, feelings, social context, and experiences interact to produce a particular style of learning.

- The Neale Analysis can provide the diagnostic data to guide the teacher in devis-ing specific instruction, motivational strategies for learning, and an enriched educational milieu which will affirm the child's unique development.

## Conclusion

In summary, if we take what appears to be a simple definition of reading, such as 'read-ing is extracting meaning from text' (Gibson & Levin, 1975), we find that the underly-ing processes, acknowledged by Huey as early as 1908, are multiple and complex. Reading behaviour mirrors the processes of thinking in a coordinated expression of human behaviour.

Even when one accepts a limited definition of reading as the decoding of symbols, there is such an interaction between knowledge of what the written signs represent and the extraction of a coherent message from them that the teacher must recognize the roles that language experience, grammatical structure, awareness of print conventions, and instruction all play in the decoding process.

● Reading, then, is not some commodity, acquired at school, to be tested in a stereotyped stimulus-response form. Thus the Neale Analysis is not a simple test of verbal utterances according to a list of random unrelated words.

● The Neale Analysis accepts that reading is a human lifeline which has a part to play in routine everyday transactions. Reading also fulfils some of the deepest needs of individuals, to relate to others, to express their feelings in relation to their environment, and to fashion their own verbal expression of the purposes and meaning of life. The Neale Analysis is designed to set up a dialogue between teacher and student to empathically explore ways of facilitating this acquisition of literacy in its broadest sense.

# CHAPTER 2

# Description of the Neale Analysis of Reading Ability – Revised

## Introduction

The Neale Analysis – Revised follows the style of the original (Neale, 1958) in that it consists of a set of graded passages for testing the Rate, Accuracy, and Comprehension of oral reading, and a set of Supplementary Tests for diagnostic assessments. It is both an attainment test and a diagnostic test. It can be used to assess reading progress objectively in the primary school and to obtain structured diagnostic or clinical observations of an individual's reading behaviour both at primary levels and beyond. Both uses should lead to improvements in planning programmes of work and more appropriate teaching strategies.

## Test Materials

The Neale Analysis – Revised consists of three parts:
*The Manual:* this contains detailed information concerning the development, description, administration, and scoring of the test.
*The Reader:* this contains all the narratives that might be used to 'hear' the child read. They are organized according to their form, i.e. Form 1 and Form 2, or the Diagnostic Tutor Form. They are colour coded for easy selection. Additionally, Supplementary Diagnostic Tests are included at the end of each Form.
*The Individual Records:* these consist of colour coded individual scoring sheets for recording the running analysis of errors for each passage that the child reads, the answers to the comprehension questions, and the time taken to read each passage. Additional qualitative information concerning the child's reading behaviour is also recorded here.

## The Demonstration Cassette – a Guide to Successful Testing

A Demonstration Cassette has been produced to help test users familiarize themselves with the procedure for administering the standardized Forms 1 and 2. Because the administration procedure involves several activities – listening to a child read aloud, prompting where necessary, and recording reading errors, comprehension and the time taken to read each passage – it is important to be thoroughly conversant with the test procedure before using the Neale Analysis – Revised. The Demonstration Cassette illustrates good practice in administering the Neale Analysis and highlights some of the pitfalls that may occur. The recording includes extracts from test sessions with three children of differing reading abilities, and a commentary describing and linking the various extracts.

Before listening to the cassette, test users should read through the instructions for administering Forms 1 and 2 on page 11 of this Manual.

## Main Features

The assessment of the child's reading skills with the Neale Analysis is structured, not in a formal way, where readers could be threatened with a pass or fail, but rather as an interaction between a child reading and a sympathetic person listening.

● The test material is presented as a book, a symbol of literacy. The book comprises short, graded narratives, each one constructed with a limited number of words and having a central theme, action, and resolution.

● Pictures accompanying each narrative are designed to set the scene rather than to illustrate details. As in the original Neale Analysis, the pictures serve three practical purposes: they transform the test material into a more appealing format, they help readers switch readily from one train of thought to another as they progress from narrative to narrative, and in some children they provoke spontaneous conversation which may be helpful to the test administrator making recommendations for tutoring and for selecting reading materials.

● Forms 1 and 2 are two standardized parallel forms of six graded passages of prose forming a continuous reading scale for children aged from 6 to 12 years. Each passage is a complete narrative written according to the interests and age level to which it is assigned.

● The Diagnostic Tutor Form, while parallel in style and grading to the standardized forms, is not supplied with norms. It includes extra passages at the three lowest levels. Miscue analysis, criterion-referenced assessments, diagnostic teaching, etc. would be best undertaken with this form. An Extension Passage is also provided for advanced work with very proficient primary-aged readers or those in secondary school.

● There are four comprehension questions for the first passage in each form, and eight comprehension questions for the subsequent graded passages. The questions are administered after the oral reading of each passage.

● Comprehension is assessed in terms of questions that tap a child's use of all contextual cues – pictures, prompts, and the language of the questions. They test the immediate recall of the main idea of the narrative, the sequence of events, and other details, and some limited inference.

● An important change in procedure is incorporated into the Neale Analysis – Revised which is expected to improve the validity of measures obtained from the Comprehension subscale. Children are now to be given a practice passage to start on so that they know exactly what is expected of them in the test. It enables them to set up a 'strategy for response' or appropriate 'reading set'. The Practice Passages have been written at two distinct levels. Independently, they offer the opportunity for diagnostic information to be obtained, even if the child is unable to proceed to the Level 1 passage in either test form.

● Accuracy in reading is assessed by recording the child's errors. The term 'errors' is retained for inaccuracies in reading which in some current models of reading are termed 'miscues'. In the Neale Analysis, these errors are viewed as the frequency count of difficulties that are exhibited in a child's oral reading. They are used for normative purposes to obtain an objective measure of the accuracy with which a child recognizes words. Additional categories of errors are defined for the test administrator to use in qualitative analysis of semantically or syntactically acceptable miscues.

- Unlike the miscue technique, the Neale Analysis allows the test administrator to correct the children's errors up to a certain limit as they read. These 'prompts', or corrections, facilitate the flow of oral reading and help the reader to maintain understanding. The children's confidence in their skill is boosted, and by supplying the correct word the test administrator prevents them from reinforcing incorrect decoding responses.

- Standardized scores are provided for Form 1 and Form 2 — percentile ranks, stanines, and reading ages for Accuracy, Comprehension, and Rate of Reading.

- Individual Records are provided for recording all details relating to each child's reading performance. One section allows for the administrator's running record to be made as the child reads each passage. Another section provides a check list for a qualitative appraisal of the child's reading behaviour and personal characteristics, while the final section facilitates a summary of the objective scoring and other details leading to the administrator's recommendations.

- Supplementary Diagnostic Tests are provided for the administrator to sample performance on component reading skills. They can be used on their own, or in any order, in conjunction with a practice passage or the particular form being employed for testing. This assembly of tasks does not imply an hierarchical model of the reading process, but rather a range of tasks that could confirm or eliminate possible areas of difficulty, e.g. phonemic awareness, memory for regular and irregular word patterns, and auditory discrimination.

- The Neale Analysis — Revised may be used to measure the reading ability of most children between the ages of 6 and 12 years, although students beyond these years and some adults can be tested on appropriate passages to obtain a general level of reading ability and for diagnostic purposes.

- Administration time for the test varies, depending upon the age and ability of the individual, and according to the nature of the objectives for testing and the administrator's experience with the materials. In general, a standardized assessment takes 20 minutes.

# CHAPTER 3

# Administering and Scoring the Standardized Forms

## Guidelines for Administration

### Selecting the Appropriate Test Form

One of the basic reasons for testing is to increase the accuracy, range, and depth of observations of a child's reading performance, and to elucidate the factors or experience that have a direct bearing upon the child's attainment. The standardized test frees the teacher considerably from a subjective choice of materials and provides a statistically derived set of standards for making judgements. It also systematizes the search for the underlying factors — namely the antecedents and correlates — of the child's attainment in reading. The test user should always be clear about the reason for testing, and be certain that the type of assessment matches the objective, so that the appropriate form of the Neale Analysis — Revised is administered.

The administrator must consider whether an informal or semi-structured appraisal of a child's reading would suffice through the administration of the Diagnostic Tutor or the Supplementary Diagnostic Tests, or whether a formal standardized test with Form 1 or Form 2 is necessary. The following may serve as a preliminary check list of objectives for clarifying whether one intends to:

● classify children for appropriate learning experiences: for example, children who are fluent readers within the first year of school might usefully be identified for enrichment activities, library work, writers' groups and so on, while those who are naïve learners are given basic tuition;

● diagnose specific strengths and weaknesses in order to improve the effectiveness of the instructional process: thus, computer-assisted instruction may be instigated to provide individual repetitive exercises in relation to the errors obtained from the child's test record;

● test whether there has been transfer of learning skills from general instruction in the classroom, or from individual special needs tutoring (this would apply particularly to word attack skills, the sequencing of ideas, and syntactic rules);

● provide normative data on a child's current level of reading skills while identifying weaknesses and strengths in information processing, i.e. speed, fluency of decoding, and comprehension of oral reading;

● probe a child's interests in reading in a way that stimulates the spontaneous expression of attitudes and reveals idiosyncratic use of oral language;

● establish a working relationship at the start of tutoring, either individually, or in small groups of children with special needs.

Table 1 provides guidance in the selection of the appropriate test form for the different testing objectives (see following page).

**Table 1:** *Selecting the Appropriate Test Form*

| Objectives | Test form to use |
|---|---|
| Identify children suited to particular programmes of work | Form 1 or Form 2 |
| Diagnose specific strengths and weaknesses | Form 1 and Form 2, Diagnostic Tutor Form, Supplementary Tests, Extension Passage |
| Test for transfer of learning skills from general or special needs teaching | Form 1 or Form 2 |
| Obtain normative data | Form 1 or Form 2 |
| Probe reading interests | Diagnostic Tutor Form |
| Establish rapport for future teaching | Practice Passages, Diagnostic Tutor Form, Extension Passages |

## General Conditions for Testing

While the Neale Analysis – Revised is simple to administer and score, it is necessary to study the instructions and the scoring before attempting to use the data for *normative* purposes. Particular attention should be paid to the comprehension questions, permissible answers and the separate error categories.

A demonstration cassette has been produced to help test users familiarize themselves with the administration procedure. Teachers should listen to the cassette *after* they have read through the instructions for administering Forms 1 and 2 given on page 11 of this manual. It is also a good idea to practise administering the test before conducting any real test sessions.

In all cases, the maximum amount of diagnostic information can be obtained if the test administrator:

- ensures that the child is able to attend to and understand directions, and is able to formulate the necessary responses;
- is thoroughly familiar with the use of norms and the interpretation and reporting of scores;
- understands that in any test there are limitations to the norms;
- has some knowledge of current approaches to the assessment and teaching of reading.

The surroundings should be quiet and free from distracting influences. Other children should not be present. Light should be good, and it is generally advisable to check whether the child usually wears spectacles for reading; for some young children, it may be necessary to see that their spectacles are clean and worn properly for the reading assessment.

The test administrator should remember to have the Manual open at page 12 for administering the test. *These directions should be read exactly as written for the standardized testing, but spoken in a natural, friendly manner.*

## Essential Equipment

Before the assessment session begins, the administrator should have ready the Reader containing the passages, the appropriate Individual Record for the form to be used, a pencil, writing paper for any possible supplementary testing and a stop-watch or digital watch with seconds display. (Passages are timed in seconds only; it is not necessary to record tenths of seconds.) A cassette recorder is particularly useful for subsequent verification of the errors made in reading.

### Establishing Rapport

Before beginning the test, the administrator should put the child at ease. This could be accomplished by:

- general conversation, e.g. relating to home, friends, games, hobbies, interests; such conversation may offer qualitative information on background of reading, language, and attitudes to school and reading;
- explaining in matter-of-fact, but encouraging, terms what is expected in the assessment, namely:
  - **a**  that the child will be asked to read several short stories aloud and answer some questions about them;
  - **b**  that help will be given with difficult words;
  - **c**  that note will be taken of the rate of reading, although reading accurately is more important than reading quickly;
  - **d**  that the child will be asked which passages were preferred;
- administering either Practice Passage One (for naïve readers, 5 to 7 years of age approximately) or Practice Passage Two (for readers above 7 years of age). Note that as these practice passages are alternatives, only one set of recording boxes is provided on the Individual Record. Use the standard directions for administering the test in a positive and encouraging manner.

## Directions for Administering Forms 1 and 2

### Where to Start Testing

In all instances start with the appropriate Practice Passage. Then proceed as follows:

1  Begin testing from the first passage of the scale for all children, unless the pupil being tested is a more competent reader, and a 'basal' level can be established by starting with a passage where the child makes no more than two errors.

2  If the child makes more than two errors on this starting passage, do not give the comprehension questions. Return to the preceding passage and apply the same limit. This process should continue until the errors are fewer than two or the Level 1 passage is reached.

3  If the limit is met, full credit is given for the prior passages, which are assumed to have been read without error.

### When to Stop Testing

1  Present each passage and the accompanying comprehension questions until the reader reaches a passage in which 16 errors are made. In the case of Passage 6, stop when the child has made more than 20 errors.

2  If the child makes the maximum number of permissible errors (i.e. 16 errors on Passages 1 to 5, or 20 errors on Passage 6), *give* the comprehension questions.

**3** If the child *exceeds* the number of permissible errors on a particular passage, *do not ask* the comprehension questions for that passage. The ceiling for Accuracy, Comprehension, and Rate of Reading has already been reached.

**4** In practice, it is found that a child making more than 12 errors in a passage is unlikely to master the next passsage. In such a case one would not proceed to the next level if it seemed likely that to do so would cause undue stress.

**5** In the case of a child between six and seven years of age who has found the Practice Passage difficult and has made between 8 and 10 errors on Passage 1, do not proceed to Passage 2 but explore word attack skills. Conclude the session on a note of success by using a simple passage from the Diagnostic Tutor and by discussing library and book activities that might be appropriate.

**6** Rather than finishing abruptly and so conveying a sense of failure to a struggling reader, conclude the test with a comment such as the following: 'That's fine, I think we shall stop here. What was that story about?' or 'How do you think it was going to end?' or 'Well done! Let's finish this story off together.' Needless to say no further scoring will take place once such a strategy has been adopted.

**7** Remember to ask the child which narratives were preferred, and respond with a positive interest to the choices.

### Procedure for Testing

Before opening the Reader, say:

> **'Here is a short story book. I should like you to read some of the stories, and tell me which story you like best.'**

Then open the Reader at the appropriate Practice Passage and say:

> **'Read this story to me first so that you understand what we are going to do. I shall help you with any words that you don't know. I shall also ask you some questions about the story when you finish.'**

There is no need to record the time taken to read the Practice Passage, but a note should be made on the Individual Record of the child's errors and the responses to the comprehension questions. Follow the procedure for prompting the child and recording errors and comprehension described below.

Having asked the questions on the Practice Passage and established that the child understands what is expected, turn to the appropriate passage for beginning the test and continue:

> **'Look at this picture and then read the story to me. If you come to a hard word, try it aloud by yourself before I help you. I am going to record the time it takes you to read, but it is more important to read carefully and to remember what you read. At the end I shall ask you some questions, so try to remember the story as you read it.'**

A glance at the picture is all that is necessary. If it is protracted, simply point to the first word and *as the child says the word, start timing.*

There is no need to repeat the above instructions as the child proceeds from one passage to the next, but it may be necessary to do so in the case of a child who is diffident or appears anxious.

## Prompting the Child

In general, it is advisable not to correct or prompt to the extent that the administrator intrudes on the fluency of the child's reading.

When a child reads a word wrongly but continues with the text, prompt with the correct word so that comprehension is maintained, and mark the text 'Sub' (substitution). (See below for help on how to record and categorize errors.)

When a child hesitates, offer the correct word after about five seconds.

When a child attempts to decode phonetically, offer the correct word if it is not achieved within six seconds.

It is not necessary to time these pauses during the test session but simply to become accustomed to the lapse of time normally required.

Do not prompt too quickly, nor allow gaps to develop in which comprehension may be lost as the child tries to decode a single word. Adjust the speed of prompting to the rate at which the child reads.

When children hesitate at words like 'by', 'box', 'bed', 'bear', 'beat', 'began', 'pet', 'play', 'pool', 'part', 'pull', 'dog', 'gave', 'gull', 'quickly', 'during', 'brief' and 'buried', where it is possible that the initital letter is a source of confusion, it is wise to encourage them to attempt the first sound rather than to prompt in the usual way.

## Recording Errors

The following example shows how errors should be recorded on the Individual Record.

**Kitten** (Level 1)

blayk (Mis)               h~ (Ref.)        little (Add) Kitty (Sub) (Om)
A black cat came to my house. She put her/ kitten by the door. Then she went away.
(Om)
Now I have her baby for a pet.                               (26 words)

A good rule to follow is to observe and record accurately at the time of reading, without attempting to categorize the errors simultaneously. The accuracy score depends on this procedure being rigidly adhered to, and adequate spacing of the narrative on the Individual Record allows for the exact recording of what is said (or omitted) above the text.

The precise categorization of errors and scoring should be carried out when the child has completed the test, and the qualitative assessment on page 8 of the Individual Record filled in, while the performance is still fresh in the administrator's memory. The use of a cassette recorder will facilitate this process.

When children correct themselves, ignore the initial error (i.e. do not mark it as an error unless the self-correction is wrong, in which case score it as a substitution error).

It will be noted that repetition, disregard of punctuation and hesitations, which some tests treat as errors, are not penalized, although it is advisable to note these for their diagnostic value.

## Recording Time

Timing begins as the child says the first word of the passage. *As the last word of the passage is read, stop the watch and record in seconds, in the appropriate place on the Individual Record, the time taken to read the passage.

## Recording Comprehension

Ask the Comprehension Questions immediately the child has finished reading the passage.

If the number of errors made by the child *exceeds* 16, or 20 in the case of passage 6, do *not* give the comprehension questions for that passage. The ceiling for Accuracy, Comprehension and Rate of Reading has been reached, and testing should stop.

If, however, the child makes *exactly* the permitted number of errors on a particular passage – i.e. 16 errors on passages 1 to 5, or 20 errors on passage 6 – the Comprehension Questions should be given.

The questions should take the form given on the Individual Record and although answers in the child's own words are acceptable, *make sure that the sense is identical with that of the answers supplied in the Answer Key on p.62 of this Manual.*

Where 'Boy/Girl' appears in the question, use the gender suited to the child.

It has been found that opening and closing the Reader during questioning destroys the continuity of the assessment. It is preferable to leave the Reader open at the narrative just read, but if it is obvious that children are returning to the text, remind them that they should try to remember the answers. If, after this reminder, children continue such a strategy, this should be noted.

The child may elaborate on an answer, and give information that is relevant to other questions. Exercise discretion in giving credit for answers supplied in this way and employ a flexible approach to the rest of the questions ensuring that all the questions are covered. A 10 to 12 second pause may be needed to give the child time to recall the answer.

Where the child does not know the answer or replies incorrectly, move on to the next question *without supplying the correct answer.*

Mark the boxes on the Individual Record in such a way that doesn't convey success or failure to the child. Crosses may be quite off-putting so try using an oblique or a horizontal line, and instead of a tick try using a number 1 or a vertical line.

## Categorizing the Errors

It is important to record accurately the number of errors, or prompts, and their type; i.e. mispronunciations, substitutions, refusals, additions, omissions and reversals. Before testing begins, the administrator should be familiar with these error categories and their meanings.

### *Mispronunciations: Decoding Errors*

Mispronunciations are words that are wrongly pronounced or distorted and only partially decoded. They should be transcribed phonetically on the Individual Record. They afford information on the way a child attempts to decode the main features in the word. Note that normal non-standard English pronunciations (e.g. 'anythink' for 'anything', 'bruvver' for 'brother') are *not* marked as errors. Dialect and accent differences are therefore acceptable. Neither would speech defects be recorded as errors where the word was clearly recognized. Apart from these exceptions, supply the correct word for each inaccuracy and record the error on the Individual Record as a mispronunciation (Mis).

## Substitutions

Substitutions are real words that are used instead of the word in the narrative, e.g. 'they' for 'then', 'her' for 'here', 'realized' for 'released'. Correct the child by supplying the right word, and record the error as a substitution (Sub).

## Refusals

If the child pauses for approximately four to six seconds, and is unable to make an attempt at a word, supply the word and record the failure as a refusal (Ref).

## Additions

Words, or parts of words, inserted in the text are recorded as additions. When more than one word is added at a single place, record it as one error only. Correct the error and record its occurrence as an addition (Add).

## Omissions

Words omitted from the text are recorded as errors. Correct the child and record the error as an omission (Om).

## Reversals

Strictly, reversals are substitutions, but they are recorded separately because of their diagnostic value, e.g. 'no' for 'on'. Correct the child and record the error as a reversal (Rev).

## Analysing the Error Categories

The categories of errors are analysed as follows:

1  A tally is made of the errors in each category for each passage (Figure 1).
2  The errors can be converted to percentages when the total number of errors has been recorded for all the passages that were read (Figure 2).
3  The percentage in each category will indicate the type of error that has occurred most frequently and should be noted for follow up teaching.

**Figure 1:** *Error Count by Category for a Single Passage*

| | | | | | | PASSAGE TOTALS | |
|---|---|---|---|---|---|---|---|
| Mispronunciations | Substitutions | Refusals | Additions | Omissions | Reversals | Comprehension: | |
| 3 | | 5 | | | | Errors: | 8 |
| | | | | | | Time: | |

**Figure 2:** *Total and Percentage Errors by Category*

| ERROR COUNT | | | | | | | |
|---|---|---|---|---|---|---|---|
| | Mispronunciations | Substitutions | Refusals | Additions | Omissions | Reversals | Total count |
| Error count (brought forward) | 6 | 2 | 12 | | | | 20 |
| % of total count* | 30% | 10% | 60% | | | | *$\frac{\text{Error count}}{\text{Total count}} \times 100$ |

## The Summary Record

The front page of the Individual Record provides for the recording of details of the child's raw scores, percentile ranks, stanine scores and reading ages, in addition to the qualitative assessment and the examiner's recommendations. Figure 3 is an example of a completed front page of the Individual Record for Karen Bowman, although most teachers will require only some of this information.

**Figure 3:** *Sample of Front Cover of Individual Record Form 2*

| Name | *Karen Bowman* | | School | *Sutton Primary* | | |
|---|---|---|---|---|---|---|
| Date of birth *2.6.79* | Date of testing *25.7.88* | Age at testing *9* Yrs *1* Mths | Year group *J2* | Language(s) at home *English* | | |
| Test administrator | | | Class teacher *Ms. Robertson* | | | |

### RAW SCORE SUMMARY

| Passage | Number of words | RATE Time in seconds | ACCURACY Maximum score | –(minus) | Number of errors | = Accuracy score | COMPREHENSION Number of correct answers |
|---|---|---|---|---|---|---|---|
| Level 1 *Kitten* | [ 26] | 12 | 16 | – | 0 | = 16 | 4 |
| Level 2 *Surprise Parcel* | [ 49] | 17 | 16 | – | 2 | = 14 | 7 |
| Level 3 *Circus* | [ 71] | 82 | 16 | – | 9 | = 7 | 5 |
| Level 4 *Dragon* | [ 91] | 126 | 16 | – | 15 | = 1 | 1 |
| Level 5 *Brigantine* | [~~116~~] | | 16 | – | | = | |
| Level 6 *Everest* | [~~137~~] | | 20 | – | | = | |
| Total number of words in passages read [*237*] | | Total time *237* | ////////// | | | | |
| TOTAL RAW SCORES | | † 60 | ////////// | | | 38 | 17 |

$$\dagger \text{ Words per minute} = \frac{\text{Total number of words}}{\text{Total time}} \times 60 = \frac{237}{237} \times 60$$

- **Rate:** use only those passages that were *actually read* by the child.
- **Last passage read:** where the permissible number of errors is exceeded do not use that passage in *any* calculation.
- **Basal Level:** credit earlier passages fully for Accuracy (i.e. write in 16 for passage score) and Comprehension (i.e. 4 for Level 1 and 8 for Level 2 and above).
- **Directions for administering and scoring this form may be found on page 9 of the Manual.**

### STANDARDIZED SCORE SUMMARY

| | RATE | ACCURACY | COMPREHENSION |
|---|---|---|---|
| READING AGE | 8:06 | 7:08 | 8:07 |
| EQUIVALENT AGE RANGE | 7:00-10:00 | 6:04 -9:00 | 7:02-10:00 |
| NATIONAL PERCENTILE RANK | 38 | 17 | 34 |
| STANINE | 4 | 3 | 4 |

### ERROR COUNT

| | Mispronunciations | Substitutions | Refusals | Additions | Omissions | Reversals | Total count |
|---|---|---|---|---|---|---|---|
| Error count (brought forward) | 9 | 13 | 3 | 1 | — | — | 26 |
| % of total count* | 34 % | 50% | 11% | 4% | | | *$\frac{\text{Error count}}{\text{Total count}} \times 100$ |

Summary and Recommendations: Analysis of K's errors reveals she uses overall passage cues to make substitutions which are appropriate semantically and syntactically. But sometimes she loses meaning and has made the maximum number of errors on her age-appropriate passage. K does not have a strong sense of sound-symbol relationships: she often attends to initial letters only. General teaching approach: continue to encourage use of linguistic cues; provide practice in decoding words, focusing on middle and final letters and syllables.

# Raw Scores from the Neale Analysis – Revised

Raw Scores for Accuracy, Comprehension and Rate are based on the passages that the child has read with exactly, or less than, the permissible number of errors. Where a basal level has been established, the comprehension and accuracy scores are also based on the passages below the basal level that were not actually read. Since the practice passages are intended to help the child understand what the test involves, they are not included in the Raw Score calculations.

> **The permissible number of errors is 16 for passages 1 to 5, and 20 for passage 6.**

## Accuracy Raw Scores

The highest possible score for each of the first five passages is 16 and for the last passage 20. This gives a scale of 100 points covering the six narratives.

The Raw Score for Accuracy is obtained as follows:

- Calculate the score for each passage by subtracting the number of errors from 16 in the case of passage 1 to 5, and from 20 for passage 6. Enter these values in the appropriate place on the Individual Record.
- For the **last passage read by the child**, if *more* than the permissible numbers of errors have been made, no score is calculated.
- If a **basal level** has been established, give full credit – i.e. 16 points – for the passages below that level that were not read.
- Add together the passage scores to obtain an Accuracy Raw Score for the test out of 100 points. Enter this value in the Raw Score Summary on the front page of the Individual Record.

An Accuracy Raw Score might be made up in the following way. A child, beginning at level 2 (established as basal level) is assumed to make no errors on passage 1, and so obtains 16 points. Two errors are made on passage 2, which gives a score of 14 points. On passage 3, nine errors are made which gives 7 points, but on passage 4, fifteen errors are made which gives a score of just 1 point. Testing now ceases, since it would be unlikely that the next passage would be read with fewer than sixteen errors. Totalling these points gives an accuracy score for this child of 38 (Figure 4).

## Comprehension Raw Scores

There are four comprehension questions for passage 1, giving a maximum possible score of 4 points, and eight questions for each of the passages 2 to 6; the highest possible score on these passages is therefore 8, which gives a total for the test of 44.

The Raw Score for Comprehension is obtained as follows:

- Give one point for each comprehension question that the child has answered correctly up to the passage on which the ceiling of reading errors is reached. Record the number of correct answers for each passage in the appropriate place on the Individual Record.
- For the **last passage read by the child**, if the number of permissible errors has been *exceeded*, the comprehension questions are not given and no score is calculated. The prompting and the correction of errors beyond 16 words, or 20 on passage 6, will tend to represent children's listening comprehension within the established limits of the test rather than their reading comprehension.

**Figure 4:** *Raw Score Summary*

| | | RATE | ACCURACY | | | | | COMPREHENSION |
|---|---|---|---|---|---|---|---|---|
| Passage | Number of words | Time in seconds | Maximum score | –(minus) | Number of errors | = | Accuracy score | Number of correct answers |
| Level 1 *Kitten* | [ 28] | — | 16 | – | | | – 16 (credit) | 4 (credit) |
| Level 2 *Surprise Parcel* | [ 49] | 17 | 16 | – | 2 | | – 14 | 7 |
| Level 3 *Circus* | [ 71] | 82 | 16 | – | 9 | | – 7 | 5 |
| Level 4 *Dragon* | [ 91] | 126 | 16 | – | 15 | | = 1 | 1 |
| Level 5 *Brigantine* | [128] | — | 16 | – | | | = | |
| Level 6 *Everest* | [129] | — | 20 | – | | | = | |
| Total number of words in passages read [ 211 ] | | Total time 225 | ///////// | | | | | |
| TOTAL RAW SCORES | | + 56 | ///////// | | | | 38 | 17 |

**RAW SCORE SUMMARY**

$$+ \text{ Words per minute} = \frac{\text{Total number of words}}{\text{Total time}} \times 60 = \frac{211}{225} \times 60$$

• **Rate:** use only those passages that were *actually read* by the child.
• **Last passage read:** where the permissible number of errors is exceeded do not use that passage in *any* calculation.
• **Basal Level:** credit earlier passages fully for Accuracy (i.e. write in 16 for passage score) and Comprehension (i.e. 4 for Level 1 and 8 for Level 2 and above).
**Directions for administering and scoring this form may be found on page 9 of the Manual.**

● If a **basal level** has been established, give full credit for the passages below that level that were not read – i.e. 4 points for passage 1 and 8 points for each of the other passages. It is assumed that the child would have correctly answered all the comprehension questions for these passages.

● The final Comprehension Raw Score is obtained by totalling the number of correct answers for each passages. Enter this value in the raw score summary.

A Comprehension Raw Score might be made up as shown in Figure 4. The child began at level 2 and is therefore credited with the full score of 4 for level 1; 7 for level 2, and 5 and 1 respectively for levels 3 and 4 making a total of 17.

### Raw Scores for Rate

During the administration of the test, the time taken to read each passage is recorded in seconds in the appropriate place on the Individual Record. The Raw Score for Rate is based on those passages that were *actually read* with 16 or less errors, or 20 or less in the case of passage 6. However, if a basal level has been established, only a pro rata estimate of rate can be calculated. This is because an accurate raw score requires that all passages up to the child's ceiling have been read and timed.

The Raw Score for Rate of Reading is obtained as follows:

● Add together the times recorded for each passage on the Individual Record and enter this value in the raw score summary.

● For the **last passage read by the child**, if the permissible number of errors has been *exceeded*, do not include the time for this passage.

● If a **basal level** has been established, do not include the passages below that level that were not actually read, but note that only a pro rata estimate of rate can be calculated and that standardized scores for rate should be interpreted with caution.

- Obtain the actual number of words read by referring to the numbers printed in brackets alongside each passage title on the Raw Score Summary.
- Calculate the rate of words per minute by using the formula provided on the front page of the individual record: divide the total number of words read by the total time and multiply by 60.

A Raw Score for Rate of Reading might be made up as shown in Figure 4: the child has reached ceiling on passage 4 (Form 2) with 15 errors. The child began at passage 2 so the total number of words read by the end of this narrative is 211, and the time taken for reading the three passages is 225 seconds. This results in a Raw Score for Rate of Reading of fifty-six words per minute (to the nearest whole number). The Raw Score for Rate is entered in the appropriate place in the Raw Score Summary on the Individual Record.

## Standardized Scores from the Neale Analysis – Revised

Once the Raw Score Summary has been completed, these scores can be converted to standardized scores using the Conversion Tables provided in this Manual.

The Neale Analysis – Revised provides three kinds of standardized scores: percentile ranks, stanines, and reading ages for the Rate, Accuracy, and Comprehension Raw Scores. Separate norms are provided for both of the standardized forms. Each type of standardized score is discussed briefly below, as well as the procedure for obtaining the appropriate score from the Conversion Tables. Note that if a basal level has been established, scores for rate can only be estimated (see page 18). In this case, standardized scores for rate should be interpreted with caution.

### Percentile Ranks

The raw scores for Rate, Accuracy, and Comprehension can be converted into percentile ranks with the appropriate Conversion Tables. Percentile ranks are expressed in terms of the percentage of persons in the standardization sample who fall below a given raw score. For example, if a girl obtained a percentile score of 68 it means that she scored as well as or better than 68 per cent of the students in the reference group for that age. Again, if a boy earned a percentile score of 36, it means that 64 per cent of the individuals of his age group who took the test scored above him.

Percentile ranks should not be confused with the familiar 'percentage scores' – the latter are like raw scores, expressed in terms of the percentage of correct items. Percentile ranks are converted scores or standard scores that are expressed in terms of the percentage of persons passing.

Percentile ranks are easily understood especially when test results are being discussed with parents. Even a person who thinks of percentiles as being equally spaced (which they could not be unless the same number of persons obtained each raw score) can understand something about these scores if he knows only that a percentile rank is a statement of the percentage of cases in a specified group who fall at or below a given score value. On the other hand interpercentile distances are not equal, sometimes leading to over-emphasis of differences near the median (mean) and an under-emphasis of differences near the extremes (see Figure 5). For this reason it is probably always safer to see a percentile rank as falling within a range. The 'true' percentile rank for any given child is likely to fall within a range either side of the obtained ranking. This range has not been reported here, as to do so would add to the proliferation of scores while contributing little to the information already provided by the Neale Analysis – Revised. However, in reporting results, the idea that a percentile rank falls within a range of score values, as does the Reading Age, may be conveyed by using Stanine Scores which are described in the following section.

To obtain a percentile rank from a raw score use the Conversion Tables and the following procedure:

**1**  Check that the raw scores for Accuracy, Comprehension, and Rate are correct according to the scoring procedures outlined in this Manual.

**2**  Check that you are using the appropriate conversion table for the test form that you have administered (i.e. Form 1 or Form 2; note that the shaded tables relate to Form 2) and for the aspect of reading that has been tested (i.e. Rate, Accuracy, or Comprehension).

**3**  Check the age of the child and locate the appropriate age table.

**4**  Locate the child's raw score, and read from that value to the right to obtain the percentile rank.

**5**  Record this score in the appropriate place on the front page of the Individual Record.

**Figure 5:** *Relationship between Selected Scores in a Normal Distribution*

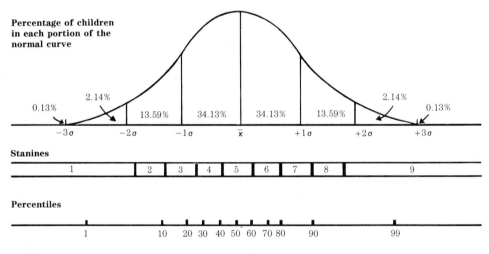

$\bar{x}$ = mean
$\sigma$ = standard deviation

## Stanines

Stanines are reported in the same tables as those for percentile ranks. Stanines really represent broad units, or bands of values, with each stanine equal to approximately one-half of a standard deviation in width and the mean being the mid-point of the fifth or middle stanine. Normally distributed scores are divided into nine units of varying size. The nine units of this scale have essentially equal distances along the base line of the curve of normal distribution. A stanine of 8 is far above the mean (5) as a stanine of 2 is below the mean. Stanines are useful for reporting differences in broad general terms. Figure 5 shows the relationships that exist in a normal distribution among the two types of standardized scores, percentile ranks and stanines.

In general, stanines have the advantages and limitations of other broad unit scores. It is unlikely that a person's score is many units away from their true score, but a test interpreter is perhaps more likely to place undue confidence in the accuracy of an obtained score. However, stanines may not allow fine enough discriminations to be made between the performances of different pupils to judge accurately whether teaching or special intervention has been effective.

To obtain a stanine score, use the appropriate Conversion Tables and follow the procedures for obtaining percentile ranks. The stanine scores will be found in the extreme right column of these tables.

## Reading Ages

These were obtained by computing for each age group the average raw score of all the children in the sample of that age and smoothing the resulting curve of average raw score against age. It was found that the curve levelled off, indicating that increases in performance with age were smaller for the older age groups. This suggests a model of reading acquisition in which learning, especially for accuracy and rate of reading, increases incrementally during the primary years and then levels out in later years. According to this model, accuracy and rate of reading would show no improvement beyond a certain point; and indeed it is probably true to say that later improvements in reading ability take place in the speed of silent reading and the more advanced comprehension and study skills aspects of reading which the Neale Analysis – Revised does not address.

For each raw score point, the Equivalent Age Range was established by taking one standard deviation above and one below the corresponding Reading Age. This gives a band around each Reading Age for which there is a 68% or approximately a 2 in 3 probability that the child's 'true' reading age lies within it.

In contrast to the 1958 edition, the Neale Analysis – Revised provides separate reading age norms for Rate, Accuracy and Comprehension for each of the two standardized forms – Forms 1 and 2.

Reading ages have had considerable currency with teachers although not without criticism. However, the criticism of their use as normative scores is answered somewhat if the confidence intervals attributed to obtained scores are known. The New Zealand revision of the Burt Word Reading Test (Gilmore, Croft, & Read, 1981) emphasizes the view of such scores as estimates of reading ability and introduces the concept of 'equivalent age bands'.

The Neale Analysis – Revised has adopted a similar position. The 'equivalent age range' indicates a predicted age range for which a given score is an average accomplishment. It can be seen that nothing fixed is implied by such a score. Reading is essentially a learned behaviour, and so aspects of the process have close associations with development and age, although other considerations such as length of schooling or number of hours spent in reading instruction can be more closely associated. A low reading age need not necessarily imply any kind of immaturity or underdevelopment of a general nature, especially in the case of specific reading disability. The multiple reading ages that can be obtained from the Neale Analysis are an advantage in this respect. Such differential outcomes are themselves of considerable diagnostic value.

Another use of reading ages concerns matching reading material, classified as suitable for particular age groups, with the pupil's current level of reading attainment. Knowing the approximate reading age of the child helps avoid a lot of unnecessary frustration when a reading programme is begun.

The reading ages are obtained from the appropriate Conversion Tables according to the following procedure:

1  Check that the raw scores for Rate, Accuracy, and Comprehension are correct according to the scoring procedures outlined in this Manual.

2  Check which test form has been used (Form 1 or Form 2 – remember that the shaded Conversion Tables relate to Form 2).

3  Locate the appropriate Conversion Table for Rate, Accuracy, or Comprehension.

4  Note the reading age listed next to it and the equivalent age range.

5  Record these values in the appropriate places on the front page of the Individual Record. (See sample on page 16.)

# CHAPTER 4

# Diagnostic Tutor Form

## Description

During the revision of the Neale Analysis, a revised version of the 1958 Form B was studied in relation to the revised parallel Forms 1 and 2. An item analysis revealed overall significant correlations with these parallel forms, but less correspondence at some passage levels. Subsequently these passage levels in Form B were modified to bring them more into line with those of the parallel forms, and a seventh more extensive and complex passage added. The resulting version has been entitled the Diagnostic Tutor Form. The first groups of narratives correspond in terms of level of difficulty with those in Forms 1 and 2, and are arranged in graded steps from 6 years to 12 years. It should be noted that in the Diagnostic Tutor Form there are two alternative narratives at each of the first three levels. Conversion Tables for obtaining norms are not available for this Form, as it has not been standardized.

The Neale Analysis was termed an 'analysis' not a 'test' since it offers more than the standardized measurements of word recognition and comprehension of prose. Underlying the construction of the Neale Analysis is the view that testing and teaching are complementary functions. The more experience teachers acquire in child development and the reading process, the more skilful they will become in obtaining useful data from testing. Moreover, the more widely exposed they become to the outcomes of their diagnostic testing and the more they reflect upon the interpretation of reading behaviour – through tutoring, special needs teaching, or through following up individuals in their progress through school – the more skilled and sensitive they will become in appraising the learner and devising the most effective follow-up activities.

The Rationale on page 3 of this Manual introduced a number of points concerning assessment that apply particularly to the Diagnostic Tutor Form:

- It is necessary to be aware that complex interactions must be taken into account in any interpretation of test performance.
- Individual appraisal is important if valid information is to be obtained.
- Clinical data may have considerable bearing on the planning of reading and associated language activities initiated as a result of testing.
- Idiosyncratic ways of symbolic processing, which can create difficulties for the school beginner, can be taken into account for teaching.
- Planning, logical sequences of thought, hypothesis testing, and inferential thinking, which should have come to characterize the individual's style of learning, can be observed in testing, and appropriate steps taken to encourage the development of these skills.
- Systematic teaching of the structure of language can be complemented by provision of opportunities for individuals to express themselves in their own way, which allows them to develop their particular creativity in language expression, both oral and written.
- The varying rates at which the child deals with visual and auditory signals can be examined through oral reading, silent reading, and listening comprehension.

In summary, the Diagnostic Tutor Form can be used, modified, or manipulated in a variety of ways to provide the diagnostic data to guide the teacher in devising specific instruction, motivational strategies for learning, and a more enriched reading programme. It provides an opportunity to focus not only on the individual's weaknesses but also upon their strengths, both of which can be assessed and matched with the appropriate materials and teaching style.

## Uses of the Diagnostic Tutor Form

Reference has already been made in Chapters 2 and 3 to the general conditions and the objectives for testing. The Diagnostic Tutor Form is designed to meet all these objectives except that of providing statistically derived norms, notwithstanding its grading in relation to the Standardized Forms. A number of the ways in which this Form can be used are suggested below.

### Updating the skills of professionals

Teachers, psychologists and therapists can update their skills in differential informal assessments and the demands for rigour in standardized testing. It is well recognized that the reliability and validity of observations made in testing depend greatly upon the administrator's skill, ease, and familiarity with the tools of testing. The Diagnostic Tutor lends itself to this purpose for individual practice and for in-service training on testing and evaluation.

### Informal appraisal of reading ability

It is often useful to know the variation between a pupil's oral and silent reading comprehension, and it may also be useful to consider the relationship that these two aspects of reading have with listening skills. Teachers can use appropriate passages from the Diagnostic Tutor to check such skills without encroaching upon the use of the standardized forms for formal testing.

### 'Cloze' exercises

The teacher can use passages from the Diagnostic Tutor Form to undertake a variety of 'cloze' exercises. For example, the teacher might have a narrative copied and ask the pupils to read it silently and underline the words they do not know or write in the words that have been omitted. Alternatively, the teacher could read the story to the class, and then, in selecting individual sentences from the passages, ask the pupils to identify, from a given set of words, key words omitted from the sentences, e.g.

> They were looking for...tent pegs, poles, tadpoles.
> Jane held the man's...hand, hat, head, horse.
> John ran to get...milk, water, help.

It has been found that carrying out such 'cloze' activities with the use of a microcomputer and a simple word processing package adds an exciting and challenging dimension to these tasks for children who are slow to respond to traditional methods of instruction and tutoring.

### Informal reading inventory

A quick sampling of an individual's oral reading, with an age-appropriate passage and *without prompts*, can be made. The errors can be totalled and analysed as a percentage of the whole passage, to ascertain the individual's level of proficiency in dealing with the material. While there is no absolute criterion of proficiency that can be applied universally, the literature suggests that the accuracy of word recognition should be in the range of 95 to 99 per cent for the reader to be coping 'independently' with adequate comprehension. A passage being read with 85 to 90 per cent proficiency would suggest an 'instructional' level, and performance below such a criterion would suggest that the material was at a 'frustrational' level for the reader.

## Criterion-referenced test

Teachers will be aware of how difficult it is for test scores to reveal changes in pupils' reading levels after a period of tutoring, even with observed increases in competency in the decoding process, in sight recognition of common words, and in deriving meaning from prose passages and basic readers. Before testing an individual on a standardized form of the Neale Analysis – Revised, the teacher could take a swift survey of progress by assessing a small sample of pupils on just one of the narratives in the Diagnostic Tutor, using it as criterion-referenced test.

In a criterion-referenced test, the individual's performance is compared with some specified criterion rather than with the scores obtained by others of the same age as reflected in norm tables. Teachers are then able to set their own standards for particular pupils in mastering areas of the reading curriculum that they have been teaching. Thus a child could be taught strategies for recognizing compound words and polysyllabic words drawing on key words from a passage like 'The Fisherman', from the Diagnostic Tutor Form; for example:

look/*ing* seek/*ing*, cook/*ing*, play/*ing*
fish/er/*man* fish/*hook*, fish/*bowl*, fish/ing/*rod*

Following this tutoring, the teacher might expect that the child would read this narrative independently of prompts, with no more than, say, two or four errors, as a measure of mastery.

## Evaluation of instruction

Evaluation of instruction is essential if the teacher is to develop and refine prescriptive teaching. Test results from administering the Neale Analysis – Revised, Form 1 or Form 2, or the Supplementary Diagnostic Tutor, will reflect the reading proficiency of the individual pupil. This information can be used by the teacher to inform decisions and to shape future teaching activities. The effectiveness of these subsequent activities can be checked in a brief yet precise fashion, by using the Diagnostic Tutor. Any of the Diagnostic Tutor passages can be used to assess the tasks that the teacher sets up, e.g. oral or silent reading, shadow read-along techniques, or improvement in semantic and syntactic processing. Such a use of the Diagnostic Tutor is also likely to help the teacher or specialist make a quick but informed estimate of the appropriate time for formal retesting.

## Error analysis or miscue analysis

The original Neale Analysis (Neale, 1958) emphasized that the pattern of errors made by the children in their oral reading provides important information for determining the adequacy of the child's reading, and for planning teaching approaches. Since then, this view has been extended by the theoretical developments associated with psycholinguistics during the 1960s (Carrol, 1964; Smith, Goodman, & Meredith, 1970; Smith & Goodman, 1971). Reading tests concerned with the diagnostic teaching of reading now confirm that a main way of acquiring insight into children's reading strategies is to study their oral reading errors or miscues (Clay, 1972; Goodman & Burke, 1972; Johnson, 1979; Brennan, 1979). This view suggests that the more proficient the reader the fewer miscues he or she will make. By considering the pattern of the miscues made in the oral reading the teacher may gain more insight into possible remedial strategies. The essential aim of all of these analyses is to direct the teacher's observations to the errors being made by the child in order to identify any pattern that might be occurring at the grapho-phonic, the syntactic, or the semantic level.

Grapho-phonic errors are studied to see what degree of graphic proximity they may have to the actual print. Word analysis skills (phonic skills) and knowledge of the structural analysis of words (prefixes, roots, suffixes, contractions) all contribute to the ability to read and understand unfamiliar words. Children who are weak in this area may not be able to extract enough information from the print to make use of the context to confirm their understanding of what they are reading.

Syntactic and semantic errors may arise out of inadequate use of context to facilitate the extraction of meaning, or from over-reliance on context where the child is unable to obtain sufficient information by decoding. Context may be used at the level of the sentence being read or at the level of the whole passage. Since reading is characteristically a left-to-right procedure, the cues that the child can extract may also be either forward-acting or backward-acting, i.e. the preceding text or the following text could be influencing the reading strategy. An example of using the Neale Analysis in this way was reported by Burke (1977). A similar example, with a passage from the Diagnostic Tutor, is illustrated below:

### Ghosts (Level 4)

A (Add) cloud (Sub)        failing (Sub)                    wail (Sub)                    dreadful (Sub)
/Dark clouds blotted out the fading daylight. A mournful wailing filtered through the deserted

building. The children stopped exploring. 'Ghosts!' whispered one child. 'Nonsense!' replied the
                              curiously (Sub)                              mystery (Sub)
other. Nevertheless, they proceeded cautiously in the direction of the mysterious noise. Gathering
                                                                          Scaredly (Mis)
courage, and with mounting curiosity, they approached the old kitchen door. Scarcely daring to
            realized (Sub)                                                              (Ref)
breathe, they released the catch. Their torches searched the darkness. Immediately their anxiety
                                        crushed (Sub) whining (Sub)
turned to pity. An exhausted dog lay crouched and whimpering. A gust of wind had slammed
            when (Sub)
the door shut while the dog had been hunting for rats.                                    (93 words)

Overall, this child has made thirteen errors or miscues, but comprehension does not appear to have been impaired too much as a consequence. Most of the errors, which are Substitutions, are syntactically acceptable within the context of either the sentence or the passage. Most of these miscues have little effect on meaning, e.g. 'failing', 'dreadful', 'crushed', 'mystery', and many miscues indicate grapho-phonic information is being used, though not systematically: e.g. 'cloud' for 'clouds', 'failing' for 'fading', 'whining' for 'whimpering', 'when' for 'while', 'crushed' for 'crouched'. Only two of the miscues, 'curiously' for 'cautiously', and 'realized' for 'released', may have influenced comprehension. Contrast this effort with the error analysis taken from the clinic file of a nine-year-old boy tested under 'standardized' conditions on Form 2.

### Surprise Parcel (Level 2)

A surprise parcel for Jane *(Mis)* and Peter/*gave (Add)* arrived on Saturday. Peter looked at the/*parcel (Add)* strange *(Ref)* stamps. Jane *opened (Sub) stamp (Sub)* undid the string. Then they shouted with *daylight (Sub)(Ref)* delight. Uncle had *nest (Sub) (Ref)* sent some skates for Jane and an *(Ref) motor (Sub)* electric train for Peter. They *wanted (Sub)* were what the children had *waited (Sub)* wanted for a

long time. (49 words)

Overall, this child has also made thirteen miscues but, in contrast to the previous child, he seems content to provide a response to the reading material regardless of whether it has meaning ('parcel' for 'strange', 'stamp' for 'string', 'daylight' for 'delight', 'nest' for 'sent'). There appears to be a spasmodic response to graphic cues but the response does not go beyond word naming to confirm if the choice is appropriate. There is some suggestion in the errors of the last sentence – 'wanted' for 'were' and 'waited' for 'wanted' – that the general meaning of the passage has been retained, but this has been in the context of a number of words being prompted by the administrator using the standard test procedures. It would be reasonable to assume that, in the absence of these corrections from the administrator, this performance might well have been more confused than it was, and under normal conditions of an informal miscue analysis, this would generally be the case. *It should be remembered that when an informal analysis is carried out, the normal prompting procedure used for testing with the Neale Analysis is not to be used because it may interfere with the pattern of miscues that emerge.*

A place for recording the informal error analysis is provided on page 18 of the Individual Record. Obviously, other methods for summarizing miscues could also be used, but the method outlined contains reference to the most important cueing systems the test administrator would be looking for in the child's reading.

## The child who has difficulty with the written word

In every class, there will be some pupils who will seem to have great difficulty with the written word. Notwithstanding good intelligence, and sometimes outstanding specific talent, they take longer than their age peers to acquire the synchronization of the visual pattern of words with their own auditory sound patterns. Some children appear to find it difficult to focus on the print. Others shift their gaze spasmodically from sections of the lines of print, while others do not appear to be able to follow print when reading aloud, the feedback of their own speech interfering with the visual processing. Others demonstrate limitations and dysfunctions in auditory and visual language processing where short-term memory for sound – symbol relationships is required.

Children learn a great deal just through listening, but maturation of auditory abilities varies considerably from child to child. There may be two or three years' difference between children in their ability to discriminate between sounds with similar acoustic features. By the end of the first year of schooling, however, deficiencies in auditory and visual processing are more apparent and require specific attention since weaknesses at this stage have a deleterious effect upon learning to read. Children with no apparent serious hearing loss may still have auditory difficulties in a classroom where considerable noise may mask the teacher's instructions. In individual testing, the administrator may note a child turning to catch the sounds with the preferred ear, or watching the mouth to lip-read the sound, or asking to have directions repeated.

Attention plays a considerable part in auditory discrimination ability, particularly in detecting similarities between two or more sounds. One must therefore remember that, before assuming that there is a perceptual or auditory defect implicated in a reading difficulty, one must consider whether the child is bored, fatigued, or distracted by visual and other competing stimuli.

The omission or substitution of the initital, final, or medial sounds in a word is correlated for some children with slow progress in phonic attack to reading. Often their difficulties will be apparent in their written work. Such children require time to become habituated to the temporal order of sounds and often require motivational aids to maintain routine remedial tasks. On the other hand, they will fall miserably behind their classmates in general knowledge unless they keep pace with the information that the others are getting from their books.

Such pupils may be distinguished from those whose difficulties appear to be related to sensory impairments or neurological dysfunctions. There is now a substantial body of evidence which indicates that the major difficulty experienced by poor readers and spellers relates to reduced sensitivity and poor discrimination of the patterns of sounds of language (Wepman, 1968; Liberman, Mann, Shankweiler, & Werfelman, 1982; Jorm, 1983). Even when these children learn phoneme-grapheme relationships, they remain slow in applying such knowledge when reading. Since this excessive slowness affects comprehension, and also reduces the satisfaction children achieve from early successful reading, it is important that the teacher pursues a range of methods in observing the child's attempts at processing oral and written language. Early detection of these 'at risk' features in using language is vital for planning early intervention (Bryant & Bradley, 1985). The Diagnostic Tutor Form and Supplementary Diagnostic Tests provide ways in which relevant information may be gained by the teacher about how the child deals with sounds in words, rhyme, alliteration in speech, and the ability to understand sequences of ideas in print and oral language.

## Extension Passage

At the upper level of secondary schooling, teachers concerned with diagnostic assessments must also look at possible weaknesses in a number of aspects of reading. However, it is defeating the purposes of diagnostic testing to present the young adult with material that is clearly not related to the linguistic complexity of reading material in senior school or college studies.

An Extension Passage is therefore provided in the Diagnostic Tutor for older and more proficient readers. It was written by Neale to capture the interests of senior students and was inspired by the beautiful volume of *Doñana* by Juan Antonio Fernandez (1975). Students could follow up similar themes, e.g. conservation, ecology, adaptation in nature, the interdependence of life and species, reafforestation, restocking of waterways, primitive art and cultures, and research into unique local and international flora and fauna. The vocabulary is demanding, as are the concepts and organization of the passage where the style has been influenced by the attempt to assess reading skills at an adult level. Testing through oral reading will give insights into strategies for grouping words and ideas, for relating one concept to another, for recall of details, locating facts, and for expressing personal judgements on the theme as it relates to the local environment and the individual's knowledge and reading. The errors or miscues in reading can also be examined with the reader taking an active part in analysing them.

As in the other narratives of the Neale Diagnostic Tutor, it is useful to explore the differences between the student's rates of processing oral and written language. It has been the author's experience that a number of very able students reach the senior years of school or college and are frustrated in their attempts to obtain high grades in their written assignments. Quite frequently their ideational fluency is at variance with their ability to produce a concise, expressive statement in writing when their reading and writing skills are examined closely. There appears to be a subtle blend of spatial and visual motor difficulties when language must be organized and produced at speed for academic assignments or within examinations. This discrepancy is highlighted when the individual discusses the concepts that he or she would like to express in a piece of written work, the richness of expressive language and depth of feeling about a subject often belying a poor reputation in written language. It has been found by the author that a weakness in written language may co-exist with a deep feeling for poetry. It is only when one works in diagnosis and teaching that these specific talents and disabilities can be appreciated. The Extension Pasage may thus serve as a useful starting point for building trust between the teacher and the senior student while supplying the stimulus material for experimental teaching and retesting.

# CHAPTER 5

# Supplementary Diagnostic Tests

## Introduction

The four supplementary diagnostic tests are:

**Test 1:** Discrimination of Initial and Final Sounds
**Test 2:** Names and Sounds of the Alphabet
**Test 3:** Graded Spelling
**Test 4:** Auditory Discrimination and Blending

Tests for discrimination of initial and final sounds, recognizing the names and sounds of the alphabet, simple spelling, and word attack skills are not given routinely to every child. The Neale Analysis – Revised incorporates these tasks for individual cases where the teacher suspects that gaps occur in skills that subserve fluent oral reading. It is advisable to use the Supplementary Diagnostic Tests 1, 2, and 4 with very young children and all children who obtain very low scores on the first reading passage of any form, or who are unable to read the appropriate Practice Passage. Supplementary Test 3: Graded Spelling, should be used only with children above 7 years old and is used to explore the relationships between the child's written and oral language skills. The multi-syllabic words in the list can be used informally to assess blending and syllabification skills.

It should be noted that the Supplementary Tests sample reading behaviour and, since no test is really 'pure' in the sense of testing only one factor, further exploration should be undertaken when one suspects limitations of a child's auditory or visual processing. Again, it should be recognized that a test that may be allocated to a particular process – for example, identifying similarities in the sound endings of words – may also be used on another occasion for testing blending skills.

The four supplementary tests augment the observations that the teacher has made of a child's reading behaviour. They may point to deficiencies in instruction, weakness in auditory or visual processing, and limitations or strengths in fine motor coordination as in printing and writing. They are not standardized tests, and the teacher's observations should be supported by teach and test techniques and, where appropriate, by specific tests for spelling and auditory discrimination or for hearing and vision.

There are published packages of language-reading programmes that contain activities for developing reading skills; but the teacher or specialist can do much with games that use pictures, puzzles, rhymes, songs, and tape recorders to cultivate the child's awareness and pleasure in the sounds of language, and so work on the specific weaknesses revealed by these Supplementary Tests.

## Test 1: Discrimination of Initial and Final Sounds

The first test consists of five pictures – an apple, an egg, an insect, an orange, and an umbrella – to test the child's discrimination of the initial and final sounds in a word.

*Directions*

Say:

'Tell me what this picture is.'

If the child does not identify the item, supply that word. Then ask:

'Can you tell me just the *first* sound in that word?' Then point to the
group of letters below and say:

'Now find which one of these letters down below is the *first* sound
in the word?' (i.e. apple).

If the child does not understand the task, use his or her name and demonstrate the
initial sound (e.g. J-ane, or M-ark).

Record the child's response on page 7 of the Individual Record in the space
provided for Supplementary Diagnostic Tests.

Then point to the picture again and say:

'Tell me the name of this picture again!' When the child has named
the picture, say,

'What is the *last* sound you hear in that word?' and record the child's
response.


## Test 2: Names and Sounds of the Alphabet

Test 2 consists of the letters of the alphabet for testing the child's recognition of the
names or sounds of letters. It is important to recognize that a child starting to learn
reading is dependent upon the teaching method employed by the teacher. Thus, some
children respond to all the letters by the sound only. The letters have been arranged
in order to check quickly those letters that may be frequently confused, e.g. reversals
like 'd' and 'b', inversions such as 'm' and 'w', 'u' and 'n', confusion due to 'cloze'
effects as in 'c', 'e', and 'o', and the similarities between 'a' and 'o', and between
'i', 'j', and 'l'.

*Directions*

Say:

'What are the names of these letters?' and point to each letter in turn.
As the child proceeds to name the letters, say:

'Yes. Those are their names: tell me the names of these others.' Then
point to the rest of the letters in turn.

If the child gives the sounds of the letters rather than the name, say:

'Yes, but can you tell me the *names,* for example' [pointing to 'a'].
'This letter is "ay".' Proceed through the remaining letters. Record incorrect
responses in the appropriate place on the Individual Record.

Then say:

'Now can you tell me the *sounds* that these letters make?' Accept
the sounds that would be consistent with a child's dialect or experience of the letter
within the initial position of a word, e.g. 'a' for apple.

In recording errors of sounding and errors of naming, you should use two differ- ent styles of marking on the Individual Record: e.g. circle the sounds, and cross through or underline the names. Alternatively, the use of two differently coloured pencils might make it easier to distinguish between errors in letter sounds and errors in letter names. The lower case letters present difficulties for immature readers more frequently than capital letters.

## Test 3: Graded Spelling

The Graded Spelling Test comprises a list of simple words in which the endings, medial vowels, or initial sounds may cause confusion, and includes a selection of regular and irregular words. The spelling test may be administered in two ways, but in each case the administrator must be aware of the particular purpose of testing.

### Spelling Words Out of Context

The Spelling Test may be given orally by the administrator articulating clearly the word for the child to write. Sentence context is not provided. Confusion with consonant end- ings and medial vowels may demonstrate auditory-perceptual immaturities which can be checked further in Supplementary Test 4: Auditory Discrimination and Blending.

*Directions*

Check that the child has a pen or pencil, and some paper to write on. Then say:

> 'I want you to write down some simple words. Listen carefully, say the word yourself, and then write it.'

### Spelling Words In Context

Alternatively the Spelling Test may be used for testing performance in spelling-writing words in context. For this, you should frame a suitable sentence around the word, to ensure that children have the meaning to help them with their spelling.

*Directions:*

Say to the child:

> 'I want you to write these words. Listen to the word first, then listen to it in a sentence, say the word yourself, and then write it. For example Cat! I gave the cat some milk. Cat!'

The child says 'cat' and writes the word 'cat'.

A sample of words may be taken from each horizontal set of words. The num- ber of words drawn from each set may be varied to suit the child's competence level. Record the number of correct spellings, but stop testing when the child has made errors on four consecutive sets. A number of authors suggest techniques for categorizing spell- ing errors, which should lead to appropriate diagnostic teaching (e.g. Peters, 1975; Croft, 1983; Croft, Gilmore, Reid, & Jackson, 1981; Frith, 1980; Bradley & Bryant, 1985).

Under both conditions for testing spelling, the adequacy or inadequacy of hand- writing may also be noted when recording the errors in letter sequences. The child's written spelling list may itself demonstrate perceptual inconsistencies. Badly shaped letters, mixed spacing, inversions of letters – any of these examples may point to poor visual and spatial relationships or motor difficulties. Again, the administrator may note slowness and fragmented processing of sound-symbol relationships as the child responds to particular items. In older children such responses may also highlight a feature observed in a number of investigations, e.g. Thompson (1987), that poor readers, more frequently boys, persist with a phonic approach to spelling, relying almost exclusively on this strategy to the detriment of speedy recall of common visual patterns.

## Test 4: Auditory Discrimination and Blending

This test consists of three sets of word pairs in which the initial, medial, or ending elements of the words are manipulated. It can be used to determine whether the child is able to discriminate sounds in the medial position, the ending, or the beginning of words, or whether the child can blend the segments of the same words when they are presented orally, i.e. demonstrate auditory blending, or closure.

### Directions for auditory discrimination

It is advisable to tell the child not to watch you, to prevent lip reading. You present pairs of words and the child must indicate whether they sound the same or different.
    Say to the child:

> 'Listen and tell me if the words I say sound the same or different'.
> For example: 'Jet...jet. Are they the same or different?'
> 'Plane...train. Are they the same or different?'

If the child is successful proceed with the items from the appropriate list in the Supplementary Test.
    If the child does not succeed in the examples, say:
'Listen again' and use the child's name, for example: 'John...John', 'Debbie...Debbie'. Do not proceed with the test if the child fails to make discriminations at this stage. Record the responses and scrutinize them for patterns of errors.
    Children who demonstrate some weakness in the auditory discrimination test may also have difficulty with the auditory blending test and the analysis and synthesis of elements of words.

### Directions for auditory blending

Say to the child:

> 'Listen! I am going to say some words that are split up, and I want you to say the whole word.'
> 'For example: Sh-o-p, shop. Here's another: n-u-t, nut. Here's one more: s-el-f, self'.

Proceed with items from the appropriate lists in the Supplementary Test. Auditory discrimination and auditory blending are skills that are vulnerable to deficits in language experience or direct instruction. You should note the age of the child since most young children have some difficulties mastering all the sounds such as 'r', 's', 'l', 'th', 'gl', 'tr', 'str', and 'sl'.
    Children who have experienced intermittent hearing loss, others with a history of respiratory infections from birth, or 'glue ears', and others who have no identifiable history of sensory loss, often demonstrate confusion with 'ch', 'sh', 'sp', and 'st'. They may omit the 'l' in words like 'fold', and omit the 'd' in the past tense of words. They sometimes do not perceive differences in the endings of words like 'gives' and 'gift'.

# CHAPTER 6

# Beyond Testing

## Introduction

The assessment of a child's reading behaviour carries with it several important responsibilities. These are:

- to ensure that the testing provides a reliable and valid measure of the child's performance in relation to specified standards;
- to provide a profile of the child's performance on related components of the reading process;
- to relay the information back to the child, and to others responsible where appropriate, in a manner that emphasizes the positive features and examines any factors that may adversely affect academic learning;
- to make recommendations for follow-up action, e.g. the level of instructional material to be used, and specific suggestions for teaching aspects of word attack skills, auditory and visual memory processing, or comprehension skills.

## Some Cautions on the Interpretation of Test Results

The primary emphasis in the Neale Analysis of Reading Ability – Revised is to enable the professionals who use it to employ the assessment and appraisal procedure described in this manual with an understanding of the test's conceptual basis and of the constructs of current psychological and educational testing. It is important for test users to understand the nature of standardized scores, the errors that are inherent in any assessment device, and the effects that any deviation from the standardized conditions of testing and scoring have on the scores children achieve. Norm tables with different types of standardized score have been provided for the teacher to use in alternative ways to evaluate an individual's performance. Reasonable caution should always be used when interpreting such test scores.

A number of points should be kept in mind when using the Neale Analysis of Reading Ability – Revised. In the first place, reading is a complex skill and no test can hope to sample all the various components of the reading process. However, it is argued that a test that looks at a child's reading skills in relation to connected text or continuous prose is closer to assessing what reading is than a test that simply records oral word recognition from word lists, or one that uses multiple-choice questions after silent reading to assess comprehension, often in writing and under speed conditions. *The results of any reading test should not be considered as the definitive statement about a child's ability in this area, but rather as samples of the child's reading behaviour.* They become the basis for hypotheses that need further investigation. Under such scrutiny they may or may not be validated. Direct observation of a child's performance in completing a school assignment, additional testing, or individual teaching (especially with the Diagnostic Tutor as a starting point) may be needed before informed conclusions can be drawn.

It should also be remembered that while test scores may tell us something about the performance of a child relative to age peers, they do not give us the reason for such performance. Only a comprehensive clinical investigation of the child and his or her learning environment can help us arrive at the answers to this question.

Again, children perform poorly on tests for a variety of reasons. It is, therefore, inadvisable to conclude that a child with low scores has reading disabilities as such. Low scores may be related to any one of a number of factors, e.g. cultural or linguistic deprivation, non-English-speaking background, sensory impairments, emotional problems, or poor motivation. Without background information on a child, test scores alone should not be used to decide whether the child has reading disabilities.

## Communicating Test Results

Once an adequate understanding of the test results has been established, a further step in interpretation may be to communicate these results either orally or in writing to an appropriate person, such as a teacher, a parent, or the pupil. Care must be exercised in conveying the outcomes of testing to another person, particularly if that individual is unfamiliar with test procedures or the particular test. Lyman (1978, p. 160) recommends three important points to bear in mind when communicating test results:

1  The person who interprets test results, however casually, must understand the nature of the tests and of the test scores. If he does not understand them himself, he should not try to explain them to others.
2  As a general rule, examinees and/or parents are entitled to an interpretation of all tests taken, and in as much detail as can be understood.
3  Test interpreters should try to avoid hurting people. Wherever possible, they should aim at giving some sort of realistic encouragement to examinees.

These points should be kept in mind when communicating the results on the Neale Analysis – Revised, which was devised as a means for sympathetically appraising a range of skills related to reading. Common sense and good judgement should also guide the amount of information to be communicated.

## Using Test Results

The Neale Analysis – Revised can be used to monitor the performance of successive year groups of children, in order to determine changes in the distribution of scores; for example, to see if there are changes in average performance, or in the spread of scores. This type of monitoring, within a school, may be done by testing the whole year group, or, as the Neale Analysis is an individually adminstered test, by testing a randomly selected sample.

The Neale Analysis – Revised provides a useful comparison with other tests of reading ability, in that it tests a range of component skills in a way in which pupils, especially those performing at a lower level, find motivating. Some caution should be exercised when comparing results from individual children on different tests of reading ability. The various types of test assess different aspects of the reading process and this, alone, may result in different scores being achieved. Some tests, for example, may test word recognition only, while others require both literal and inferential comprehension – a completely different kind of skill.

Other factors affecting the scores children achieve relate to the size of the sample on which the test was standardized, and the length of time that has elapsed since the original standardization. The latter can have marked effects on test results, since the performance of the national population of school children may change over time. This effect may be illustrated by comparing the norms for the original Neale Analysis with those for the Neale Analysis of Reading Ability – Revised. The performance of older children in the 1988 sample was superior to the performance of children of the same age in the 1958 sample. This means that children in this age group who are of average ability would obtain spuriously high scores if they were tested on the original Neale Analysis because they would be being compared, not with their current peer group, but with school children of 30 years ago. Test scores from the Neale Analysis of Reading Ability – Revised will be a more realistic and therefore more useful estimate of children's current level of reading ability.

Practice effects on the Neale Analysis – Revised are low, so that children who are re-tested after a short period of time will gain very much the same score as on the first date of testing. The Neale Analysis – Revised is, therefore, particularly useful for re-testing individual children – for example those who have undertaken a special programme of study. However, it is important to be aware that Reading Ages are in fact estimates, and that the child's 'true' reading age is likely to fall within the equivalent age range given in the Conversion Tables. If children are to be re-tested, a sufficient period of time should be allowed to elapse between testing for real progress to be made, and, when evaluating the usefulness of intervention strategies, some account should be taken of the increase in scores that would be expected in the absence of any intervention. As shown in the results of the comparability study discussed on pages 59 to 60, raw scores on the Neale Analysis – Revised bear a close relationship to those on the original Neale Analysis, where there were discrepancies; these amounted to not more than one or two raw score points for Accuracy and Comprehension. However, as indicated above, some aspects of performance have improved. So, where schools have traditionally used a particular cut-off point – for example, to screen for children with special needs – they are advised to continue using the same raw score value which corresponds to that cut-off point, rather than the reading age. For example, schools that have used a Reading Age of 7 years for accuracy, which corresponds to a raw score of 12 on the original Neale Analysis, might continue to use a raw score of 12 as a cut off point, although the appropriate Reading Age would now be 5 years 5 months. Further details may be found in the next chapter under the heading Comparison between Pupil Performance on the Original Edition, and on the Revised British Edition.

## Monitoring Standards over Time

Users who wish to compare present standards of performance with levels of performance before 1988 may consider using Form 2 of the Neale Analysis – Revised since this is the old Form A slightly modified and as such offers scope for longitudinal studies.

## Tutoring from the Neale Analysis of Reading Ability – Revised

As indicated in the rationale, the author believes that two things should be taken into account when using the data from the Neale Analysis – Revised to design programmes of study.

**a** The individual, with his or her unique constitution, experiences and memories, and style of representation of the world, should be kept well in mind when a tutoring style is chosen.

**b** The active role of the learner should be emphasized both for enrichment programmes, in which language and imagery are extended, and for special help directed towards solving particular difficulties the learner may have with meaning of text or decoding skills.

The integral role of the motor system in language learning has been studied extensively by the author in designing and implementing programmes of work for exceptional children – either those who are gifted, or those with special educational needs. Diagnostic tutoring has confirmed the paramount importance of embedding concepts and strings of words in motor sequences. Expressive movement, voice and drama, singing, problem solving in mathematics, creating a story line for photographic records or a film, devising a computer program, and practical activities such as art, craft, and calligraphy have been found to be extremely successful for both enrichment and special help programmes in language and reading. Teaching in small groups has been shown both to enliven one-to-one tutoring in strategies for discriminating between the visual patterns of words, and to trigger motivation, responsive attitudes, and the active registration of the salient features of language forms. In short, the motor response links and integrates the symbols that we use to represent our many transactions with the environment.

Teachers and specialists will have preferred teaching strategies and schemes that they may wish to adapt to the learner's needs. The author, however, offers as a starting point her formula derived from clinical studies of children with specific learning difficulties and those exceptional children requiring head room and enrichment activities in advance of their age peers. It is not a prescription, but simply an easily applied guide to shaping and systematizing the tutoring. The formula leaves room for teachers to follow their own preferred schemes of reading instruction and to use other materials, but it offers a structure for the use of the results from the Neale Analysis.

The formula consists of three component acitivities: Creative Synthesis (CS), Auditory and Visual Sequencing Activities (AVSA), and Critical Examination and Evaluation of Structure (CES) of text.

## Creative Synthesis

The Diagnostic Tutor provides a means for designing a personal curriculum based on the particular knowledge and difficulties the child has demonstrated on the various passages that have been read. In a constructive relationship between the teacher and the child, there is an exploration of the meaning of the passage, the theme, alternative titles, the relationship of the theme to current events, and different ways of using the narrative to include fresh characters, new beginnings, humour, and original outcomes. The teacher helps the children to reconstruct their own interpretation of what is read. Thus, the learner, in assimilating ideas, reconstructing them and accommodating to them, acquires linguistic patterns and develops analytical skills. It is this dynamic creative synthesis of the passage that stimulates the learner and facilitates cognitive processing.

## Auditory and Visual Sequencing Activities

In learning to read, as in learning other complex skills – for example practising the scales in music, working on the component skills of leg and arm movements in swimming, and particularly in developing the direction, sequence, and flow of expressive movements in dance – learners select and attend to their errors with feedback and encouragement from the teacher. The pupil examines the visual patterns of the words in the narratives, makes comparisons and discriminations, and registers the correct correspondence between sound and visual pattern. Auditory training through speech and drama can emerge from narratives. Ways of focusing the individual's attention on the salient features of the task can be employed, such as getting the pupil to record a personal interpretation of a passage on tape and using the microphone to present the narrative as though to an audience, or developing a script emphasizing the sequence of events in the narrative. A number of the pupil's errors from the test can be chosen for 'feature' analysis with different materials and well-known teaching techniques: for example a video enlarger by which individual letters and parts of words can be separated, enlarged, and put together; plastic letter sets; magnetic letters; letter/syllable/word cards; and the Gillingham-Stillman remedial materials (1956). Kinesthetic cues can be emphasized to foster the awareness of speech sounds, the production of speech, and the writing of the correct sequence of words, for example Fernald (1943), Lindamood & Lindamood (1969), and Semel (1970).

## Critical Examination and Evaluation of Text Structure

Thirdly, there is a critical examination and evaluation of the structure of the passages, particularly the syntax, through which the material communicates its message to the reader. An examination is made of the way in which atmosphere, speed, and dramatic impact are developed in the Neale Analysis passages. Each one develops a dramatic incident, the tension being created by the contrast in length of sentences and choice of parts of speech. The resolution is often a simple statement that allows the reader a sense of identification with the main figures in the story, even if the passage causes the individual some difficulty in decoding. Discussion of these features can be related to the pupil's own style of telling a story or writing an article or succinct report.

Some critics, examining the Neale Analysis passages mainly from a linguistic point of view, do not take into account the constraints under which the author had to write. A scene had to be created with a story line that leads to a resolution of events within a limited number of words – even as few as 26! The idea, therefore, of the reader 'bridging' between the sentences to effect continuity of the story line is an essential part of the critical examination of the text. A 'conference' between teacher and pupil should lift such remedial work to the level of colleagues engaged in the broader aspects of literature.

Each narrative allows for some inference, but the demand for inferential thinking is not taken to the level of problem solving as in a cognitive exercise. A test of reading should be a test of obtaining the message from the written symbols in order to respond to it, retell it, revamp it, or transfer it to the new situation at will. Tasks that call for 'closure' in supplying specific vocabulary to the text, or which make demands upon the ability to deduce relationships of time and quantity in order to come to a solution, can be designed. A microcomputer and word processing package are useful in this respect. However, it is the author's view that these 'cloze' tasks are more appropriate within the testing of other subjects of the curriculum (e.g. mathmatics, logic, physics) and are more validly the substance of intelligence tests. Confirmation of this point of view was obtained in the factorial analyses of the original Neale Analysis in relation to tests of English, verbal and non-verbal tests of intellectual ability, perceptual motor processing, word recognition tests, and oral tests of sentence and narrative reading (Neale, 1956). However, in testing and tutoring, the teacher has the freedom to choose whether or not to extend the pupil in the use of such cognitive strategies, depending on the abilities and motivation of the individual.

Finally, with particular pupils, it is possible to extend the individual's interest to what writers now recognize is a 'contract' set up between the author and the reader. This can be related to the individual's own written language. Moreover, in examining the structure of the narratives it is useful if pupils express a preference for the type of reading material that they enjoy. It has been found that a number of children prefer to read in a specific content field, but at a level much below their actual reading attainment level. Still others, however, read and are intrigued by scientific literature that would appear to be beyond their language skills as observed in the classroom.

In summary, the structured interview with the child, together with the test scores and error analysis, provide the basis for developing a personal curriculum. The simple formula described above ensures that the child is actively engaged with the text. Though reading is a unified coordinated activity, the formula – Creative Synthesis, Auditory and Visual Sequencing Activities, and the Critical Examination and Evaluation of Structure – provides the teacher with an active routine which includes testing and teaching. Handled imaginatively, the test provides a tool for cultivating a working relationship in which both teacher and pupil explore many avenues towards an understanding and appreciation of the richness of our language and literature.

# CHAPTER 7

# Development of the Neale Analysis of Reading Ability – Revised

## The Original Edition

The Neale Analysis of Reading Ability was devised by the author in the United Kingdom during the 1950s. The original narratives were written around themes that had been chosen in pilot studies from the preferences of primary school children. Amendments were made and the stories allocated to age levels and tested on 192 children in a further pilot study. On the basis of the children's reading performance and preferences for themes, revisions were again made to the materials and further testing was undertaken on a sample of 439 children. The results were analysed and, with minor amendments, the narratives were again extensively trialled with 17 other published tests on 200 children aged nine years and 200 children aged 11 years within two factor analytic studies. The final standardization of the Analysis was then undertaken. In all, 2000 children were tested individually on either Forms A and B or Forms A and C, together with other reference tests, to obtain the normative data. The writing of all the narratives, the testing and the statistical analyses were undertaken by one person, the author, before the work was prepared for publication in 1958.

## Revision of the Neale Analysis

In 1979 a review was undertaken of the content and structure of the Neale Analysis to check the suitability of the language and the interest of the themes for present-day school children. Age samples of children were tested on the Neale Analysis, along with a number of new narratives, in an attempt to ascertain the interests of the children at different age levels. They were also asked to respond to the pictures and indicate their preferences for a story theme around the illustrations. It was found that certain themes in children's stories – such as adventures, dragons, circuses, nature – appeared to be as popular as they were in the 1950s and this gave the author confidence in retaining certain passages from the original forms. In addition, a number of informal surveys were made of professional workers using the Neale Analysis to elicit their reaction to proposed changes to the narratives and materials, and helpful criticisms on style and administration were obtained.

A number of guiding principles emerged from these surveys which suggested that, rather than drastic changes being made to the Neale Analysis, retention of the story booklet format was highly favoured by teachers. However, it was felt that some more up-to-date narratives, and more information on diagnosis, planning programmes of study and new norms should be included in any revision.

## Item Selection

### Selection of Prose Passages

All the original passages were carefully written and graded by controlling the vocabulary, the syntactic complexity, and the length of the narrative. The selection of the words in the original passages was based on word lists (Dolch, 1951) and word frequency counts from Thorndike & Lorge (1944) and Rinsland (1945), with reference to the work of Vernon (1949) and to the then unpublished study of children's oral language by Burroughs (1957). For the passages in the 1980 Australian version, on which this British edition is based, reference was made to the *Word Frequency Book* (Carroll, Davies, & Richman, 1971) to ensure that the words that were chosen were in current use by children. They were also checked against the vocabulary of contemporary basic instructional schemes of reading. Within each narrative, a number of more difficult words have been strategically employed in context to provide better discrimination among readers at that age level. In practice, it has been observed that children who are able to make good use of grapho-phonic and contextual cues are often able to guess successfully words that are beyond the level that would apply to their usual reading material. The 'average' or 'failing' reader who is tested using the Neale technique is helped with difficult words through prompts.

Each passage was written to form a complete narrative suited to the interests of the age level to which it was assigned. Some new illustrations were also developed for these revised forms, which maintained the original intention of setting the theme without supplying detailed information for the story line.

These procedures led to a revision that retained Form A from the 1958 version of the test with the exception of the second passage, 'Tom and the Milkman's Horse', in which aspects of the story line have become remote from the lives of most young children today. The second passage from Form C ('Surprise Parcel' in the 1958 version) was substituted for this story. This kept Form A virtually to the 1958 version which has been used most extensively as a reading measure in research studies in the last 25 years. It has also achieved a high level of acceptability for its reliability. Netley, Rachman, & Turner (1965) reported Form A of the Neale as having the highest test-retest reliability of the various forms of the test and recommended it as a generally highly reliable test of reading skills. This finding was confirmed by Neale, McKay, & Childs (1986) in a study undertaken alongside the Australian standardization of the revised version of the Neale Analysis. These findings confirmed the impression that the old Form A could be used as the 'standard' by which new materials could be judged. Form A thus revised was labelled Form 2.

Two modified versions of Forms B and C of the test were then developed containing many new narratives. The initial equivalence of the new narratives was arrived at by means of writing a larger pool of stories adhering to the original principles of construction used for the 1958 version. An analysis of the equivalence of these two forms with Form 2 established that the revised Form C was the most appropriate parallel form to use for routine normative purposes, while Form B could be retained as a tutoring form to provide a means for more informal diagnosis and tutoring. Thus the revised Neale Analysis consists of two parallel forms, Form 1 (the revised Form C) and Form 2 (the original Form A with minor modifications) with an associated Diagnostic Tutor Form (the revised and extended Form B).

## Selection of Comprehension Questions

The comprehension questions for each passage of prose were selected on the basis of the replies given by children in pilot studies. Eight comprehension questions follow each passage, except in the case of the first narrative where there are only four. In general, the questions follow the sequence of the narrative of the passage in order to help the children maintain sequential thought. These questions aim at assessing both literal and inferential comprehension. The list of acceptable answers was derived from the responses most commonly given by the children. In each passage there is one question that is deliberately contrived so that it will be correctly answered by the majority of the children at that age level. This is to boost the confidence of the reader.

It is possible that some of the comprehension questions measure the general level of sophistication of the readers, i.e. what they know about the world and what they have learnt. However, as Smith has put it, 'The basis of comprehension is prediction and prediction is achieved by making use of what we already know about the world by making use of the theory of the world in the head' (Smith, F., 1978, p. 87). If one accepts this viewpoint of what distinguishes between good and poor comprehension, then such questions on the Neale Analysis should elicit this discrimination effectively.

## The Analysis of Errors

It is recognized that the six categories of errors are only one set that could be used to analyse a child's errors or inaccuracies. However, it is argued that they constitute an easily understood and recognizable set of errors, which allows high reliability in objective scoring.

## The Cut-Off Point

In the Australian standardization of the revised edition, a cut-off point of 25 errors was applied for the new forms of the test, instead of Neale's original cut-off of 16 word recognition errors. It was argued that, as there was no statistical evidence for believing the old and new forms to be equivalent, children should continue to read beyond the old limit in order to establish the progressive difficulty of the passages in each form. In practice it was found that this often put pressure on children to read beyond their actual capacity, but the results reinforced Neale's original decision in 1956 to set the limit at 16 errors.

## Item Analysis

Several procedures have been adopted to ensure that the items are of appropriate difficulty, and that they discriminate satisfactorily between children of differing abilities. The analyses of the performance of the Australian standardization sample on the revised forms attempt to reflect the gradations of difficulty associated with each passage.

Tables 2A and 3A indicate that the mean errors obtained by each age group for their age-appropriate passages (the underlined values) were very similar. Passage One for children aged 6:0 to 6:11 resulted in fewer errors than average, but this was expected since it is a very short passage and was designed so that young children would experience some success. It can be seen that the mean errors for each passage decrease with age, older children making fewer errors on earlier passages than the younger children. Across the parallel forms there is also remarkable consistency in the mean errors obtained at each age level. Considering that each passage is different in theme and content, this outcome appears to reflect a satisfactory gradation in difficulty for each passage and across each form.

The approach adopted in the analysis of the difficulty level of the Comprehension questions was similar to that taken for errors made on each Passage. Means and standard deviations for questions correctly answered by each age group about their age-appropriate passages are reported in Tables 4A and 5A.

**Table 2A:** *Form 1, Revised Australian Edition – Mean ($\bar{x}$) and Standard Deviation (SD) for Errors Made in Reading Each Passage*

| Age Group | Passage Level 1 | | Passage Level 2 | | Passage Level 3 | | Passage Level 4 | | Passage Level 5 | | Passage Level 6 | |
|---|---|---|---|---|---|---|---|---|---|---|---|---|
| | $\bar{x}$ | (SD) | $\bar{x}$ | (SD) | $\bar{x}$ | (SD) | $\bar{x}$ | (SD) | $\bar{x}$ | (SD) | $\bar{x}$ | (SD) |
| Under 6 | 10 | (4) | 16 | (10) | – | – | – | – | – | – | – | – |
| 6:0 – 6:11 | 4 | (5) | 10 | (8) | 12 | (8) | – | – | – | – | – | – |
| 7:0 – 7:11 | 2 | (4) | 6 | (6) | 10 | (7) | 18 | (9) | – | – | – | – |
| 8:0 – 8:11 | 1 | (3) | 4 | (5) | 8 | (7) | 15 | (10) | 11 | (6) | – | – |
| 9:0 – 9:11 | 0 | (1) | 2 | (2) | 5 | (6) | 8 | (8) | 8 | (6) | 11 | (6) |
| 10:0 – 10:11 | 0 | (1) | 1 | (2) | 4 | (5) | 7 | (7) | 7 | (5) | 10 | (8) |
| 11:0 – 11:11 | 0 | (0) | 1 | (1) | 4 | (5) | 7 | (7) | 7 | (6) | 9 | (6) |
| 12 and over | 0 | (0) | 1 | (1) | 3 | (4) | 5 | (6) | 6 | (6) | 8 | (6) |

**Note.** *Each underlined value refers to the mean for the passage appropriate to that age group. All values are rounded to the nearest whole number.*

**Table 3A:** *Form 2, Revised Australian Edition – Mean ($\bar{x}$) and Standard Deviation (SD) for Errors Made in Reading Each Passage*

| Age Group | Passage Level 1 | | Passage Level 2 | | Passage Level 3 | | Passage Level 4 | | Passage Level 5 | | Passage Level 6 | |
|---|---|---|---|---|---|---|---|---|---|---|---|---|
| | $\bar{x}$ | (SD) | $\bar{x}$ | (SD) | $\bar{x}$ | (SD) | $\bar{x}$ | (SD) | $\bar{x}$ | (SD) | $\bar{x}$ | (SD) |
| Under 6 | 11 | (5) | 18 | (7) | – | – | – | – | – | – | – | – |
| 6:0 – 6:11 | 4 | (5) | 10 | (7) | 14 | (9) | – | – | – | – | – | – |
| 7:0 – 7:11 | 2 | (4) | 7 | (7) | 10 | (7) | 13 | (6) | – | – | – | – |
| 8:0 – 8:11 | 1 | (3) | 4 | (5) | 9 | (8) | 10 | (7) | 14 | (7) | – | – |
| 9:0 – 9:11 | 0 | (0) | 2 | (4) | 5 | (6) | 8 | (7) | 12 | (7) | 12 | (6) |
| 10:0 – 10:11 | 0 | (0) | 1 | (2) | 4 | (5) | 7 | (7) | 10 | (6) | 10 | (6) |
| 11:0 – 11:11 | 0 | (0) | 1 | (3) | 3 | (5) | 6 | (6) | 9 | (6) | 10 | (5) |
| 12 and over | 0 | (0) | 1 | (2) | 2 | (5) | 4 | (5) | 7 | (5) | 9 | (6) |

**Note.** *Each underlined value refers to the mean for the passage appropriate to that age group. All values are rounded to the nearest whole number.*

**Table 4A:** *Form 1, Revised Australian Edition – Mean ($\bar{x}$) and Standard Deviation (SD) for Total Number of Comprehension Questions Correctly Answered*

| Age Group | Passage Level 1 $\bar{x}$ (SD) | | Passage Level 2 $\bar{x}$ (SD) | | Passage Level 3 $\bar{x}$ (SD) | | Passage Level 4 $\bar{x}$ (SD) | | Passage Level 5 $\bar{x}$ (SD) | | Passage Level 6 $\bar{x}$ (SD) | |
|---|---|---|---|---|---|---|---|---|---|---|---|---|
| Under 6 | 2 | (1) | 2 | (2) | – | – | – | – | – | – | – | – |
| 6:0 – 6:11 | 3 | (1) | 3 | (2) | – | – | – | – | – | – | – | – |
| 7:0 – 7:11 | 3 | (1) | 5 | (2) | 2 | (2) | – | – | – | – | – | – |
| 8:0 – 8:11 | 3 | (1) | 5 | (2) | 3 | (2) | 2 | (2) | – | – | – | – |
| 9:0 – 9:11 | 4 | (1) | 6 | (2) | 4 | (2) | 3 | (2) | 3 | (2) | – | – |
| 10:0 – 10:11 | 4 | (1) | 6 | (2) | 5 | (2) | 4 | (2) | 4 | (2) | – | – |
| 11:0 – 11:11 | 4 | (1) | 7 | (1) | 5 | (1) | 5 | (2) | 5 | (2) | 4 | (2) |
| 12 and over | 4 | (1) | 7 | (1) | 5 | (2) | 5 | (2) | 5 | (3) | 4 | (2) |

**Note.** *Each underlined value refers to the mean for the passage appropriate to that age group. All values are rounded to the nearest whole number.*

**Table 5A:** *Form 2, Revised Australian Edition – Mean ($\bar{x}$) and Standard Deviation (SD) for Total Number of Comprehension Questions Correctly Answered*

| Age Group | Passage Level 1 $\bar{x}$ (SD) | | Passage Level 2 $\bar{x}$ (SD) | | Passage Level 3 $\bar{x}$ (SD) | | Passage Level 4 $\bar{x}$ (SD) | | Passage Level 5 $\bar{x}$ (SD) | | Passage Level 6 $\bar{x}$ (SD) | |
|---|---|---|---|---|---|---|---|---|---|---|---|---|
| Under 6 | 1 | (1) | 1 | (2) | – | – | – | – | – | – | – | – |
| 6:0 – 6:11 | 3 | (1) | 3 | (2) | – | – | – | – | – | – | – | – |
| 7:0 – 7:11 | 3 | (1) | 4 | (2) | 2 | (2) | – | – | – | – | – | – |
| 8:0 – 8:11 | 3 | (1) | 5 | (2) | 3 | (2) | 2 | (2) | – | – | – | – |
| 9:0 – 9:11 | 3 | (1) | 6 | (2) | 4 | (2) | 3 | (2) | 3 | (2) | – | – |
| 10:0 – 10:11 | 3 | (1) | 7 | (2) | 5 | (2) | 4 | (2) | 3 | (2) | – | – |
| 11:0 – 11:11 | 4 | (0) | 7 | (2) | 5 | (2) | 5 | (2) | 4 | (3) | 4 | (3) |
| 12 and over | 4 | (0) | 7 | (1) | 5 | (2) | 5 | (2) | 5 | (3) | 5 | (2) |

**Note.** *Each underlined value refers to the mean for the passage appropriate to that age group. All values are rounded to the nearest whole number.*

In these tables, the means and standard deviations for the age-appropriate passages are indicated by the underlined values. Passage 1, therefore, was written for the six-year-old group, while Passage 6 was written for the age group over 12 years old. As children younger than six years and older than 12 years were also included in the standardization sample, but not for the derivation of norms, their results are also reported.

It can be seen that few, if any, differences exist between the averages obtained by each age group on their age-appropriate passages on either form of the test. As would be expected, the means obtained for Comprehension for each passage increase progressively with age (bear in mind the fairly restricted scoring range, i.e. for Passage 1 from one to four, and for Passages 2 to 6, from one to eight).

**Table 2B:** *Form 1, Revised British Edition – Mean ($\bar{x}$) and Standard Deviation (SD) for Errors Made in Reading Each Passage*

| Age Group | Passage Level 1 | | Passage Level 2 | | Passage Level 3 | | Passage Level 4 | | Passage Level 5 | | Passage Level 6 | |
|---|---|---|---|---|---|---|---|---|---|---|---|---|
| | $\bar{x}$ | (SD) | $\bar{x}$ | (SD) | $\bar{x}$ | (SD) | $\bar{x}$ | (SD) | $\bar{x}$ | (SD) | $\bar{x}$ | (SD) |
| 6:0 – 6:11 | 4 | (5) | 9 | (7) | 13 | (5) | 15 | (3) | 16 | (2) | 20 | (1) |
| 7:0 – 7:11 | 2 | (3) | 5 | (6) | 10 | (6) | 14 | (4) | 15 | (3) | 19 | (2) |
| 8:0 – 8:11 | 1 | (2) | 2 | (4) | 6 | (6) | 11 | (6) | 13 | (5) | 18 | (4) |
| 9:0 – 9:11 | 0 | (1) | 1 | (3) | 4 | (5) | 9 | (6) | 11 | (5) | 16 | (6) |
| 10:0 – 10:11 | 0 | (1) | 0 | (1) | 3 | (3) | 6 | (6) | 8 | (6) | 12 | (7) |
| 11:0 – 11:11 | 0 | (1) | 0 | (1) | 2 | (3) | 5 | (5) | 7 | (6) | 10 | (7) |

**Note.** *Each underlined value refers to the mean for the passage appropriate to that age group. All values are rounded to the nearest whole number.*

**Table 3B:** *Form 2, Revised British Edition – Mean ($\bar{x}$) and Standard Deviation (SD) for Errors Made in Reading Each Passage*

| Age Group | Passage Level 1 | | Passage Level 2 | | Passage Level 3 | | Passage Level 4 | | Passage Level 5 | | Passage Level 6 | |
|---|---|---|---|---|---|---|---|---|---|---|---|---|
| | $\bar{x}$ | (SD) | $\bar{x}$ | (SD) | $\bar{x}$ | (SD) | $\bar{x}$ | (SD) | $\bar{x}$ | (SD) | $\bar{x}$ | (SD) |
| 6:0 – 6:11 | 4 | (5) | 9 | (7) | 13 | (5) | 15 | (3) | 16 | (2) | 20 | (0) |
| 7:0 – 7:11 | 2 | (3) | 7 | (6) | 10 | (6) | 13 | (5) | 15 | (3) | 19 | (3) |
| 8:0 – 8:11 | 0 | (1) | 3 | (5) | 7 | (6) | 10 | (6) | 13 | (5) | 18 | (5) |
| 9:0 – 9:11 | 0 | (1) | 1 | (3) | 4 | (5) | 8 | (6) | 11 | (5) | 16 | (6) |
| 10:0 – 10:11 | 0 | (1) | 1 | (2) | 3 | (4) | 6 | (5) | 8 | (6) | 14 | (6) |
| 11:0 – 11:11 | 0 | (2) | 1 | (2) | 2 | (3) | 5 | (5) | 7 | (6) | 11 | (7) |

**Note.** *Each underlined value refers to the mean for the passage appropriate to that age group. All values are rounded to the nearest whole number.*

Similar analyses of data collected during the British standardization are reported in Tables 2B to 5B. The British Standardization revealed unexpectedly low scores for Comprehension on passage 5, Form 2. (See Table 5B.) Analysis of tape recordings made for the Accuracy Study, reported later in this chapter, showed that children had difficulty sorting out the difference between 'how the young explorers were selected' (i.e. what qualities made them eligible) in Question 3, and the 'qualities shown by the young explorers in general' in Question 8. Other questions were less than straightforward in requiring more than one response for a full answer, compared with those on the corresponding passage in Form 1 which require a single response in each case.

**Table 4B:** *Form 1, Revised British Edition – Mean ($\bar{x}$) and Standard Deviation (SD) for Total Number of Comprehension Questions Correctly Answered*

| Age Group | Passage Level 1 $\bar{x}$ (SD) | | Passage Level 2 $\bar{x}$ (SD) | | Passage Level 3 $\bar{x}$ (SD) | | Passage Level 4 $\bar{x}$ (SD) | | Passage Level 5 $\bar{x}$ (SD) | | Passage Level 6 $\bar{x}$ (SD) | |
|---|---|---|---|---|---|---|---|---|---|---|---|---|
| 6:0 – 6:11 | 3 | (1) | 5 | (3) | 3 | (3) | 1 | (2) | 3 | (2) | 1 | (2) |
| 7:0 – 7:11 | 3 | (1) | 6 | (2) | 3 | (2) | 1 | (2) | 3 | (2) | 2 | (2) |
| 8:0 – 8:11 | 4 | (1) | 6 | (2) | 4 | (2) | 3 | (2) | 3 | (2) | 2 | (1) |
| 9:0 – 9:11 | 4 | (1) | 7 | (2) | 5 | (2) | 3 | (3) | 4 | (2) | 3 | (2) |
| 10:0 – 10:11 | 4 | (1) | 7 | (1) | 5 | (2) | 4 | (2) | 4 | (2) | 4 | (2) |
| 11:0 – 11:11 | 4 | (0) | 7 | (1) | 6 | (2) | 5 | (2) | 5 | (2) | 4 | (2) |

**Note.** *Each underlined value refers to the mean for the passage appropriate to that age group. All values are rounded to the nearest whole number.*

**Table 5B:** *Form 2, Revised British Edition – Mean ($\bar{x}$) and Standard Deviation (SD) for Total Number of Comprehension Questions Correctly Answered*

| Age Group | Passage Level 1 $\bar{x}$ (SD) | | Passage Level 2 $\bar{x}$ (SD) | | Passage Level 3 $\bar{x}$ (SD) | | Passage Level 4 $\bar{x}$ (SD) | | Passage Level 5 $\bar{x}$ (SD) | | Passage Level 6 $\bar{x}$ (SD) | |
|---|---|---|---|---|---|---|---|---|---|---|---|---|
| 6:0 – 6:11 | 3 | (1) | 5 | (3) | 2 | (2) | 3 | (2) | 2 | (2) | 2 | (1) |
| 7:0 – 7:11 | 3 | (1) | 5 | (2) | 3 | (2) | 3 | (2) | 1 | (1) | 2 | (2) |
| 8:0 – 8:11 | 3 | (1) | 6 | (2) | 4 | (2) | 4 | (2) | 1 | (2) | 3 | (2) |
| 9:0 – 9:11 | 4 | (1) | 7 | (1) | 5 | (2) | 4 | (2) | 2 | (2) | 4 | (2) |
| 10:0 – 10:11 | 4 | (1) | 7 | (1) | 5 | (2) | 4 | (2) | 2 | (2) | 3 | (2) |
| 11:0 – 11:11 | 4 | (1) | 7 | (1) | 6 | (2) | 5 | (2) | 3 | (2) | 4 | (2) |

**Note.** *Each underlined value refers to the mean for the passage appropriate to that age group. All values are rounded to the nearest whole number.*

## The Australian Standardization

The revised Neale Analysis (Australian Edition) was standardized on a sample of approximately 1100 children (equal numbers of boys and girls), from two Australian States, Victoria and South Australia, during the years 1981 to 1984. The sampling procedure was designed to ensure that the final sample was representative of the national population of Australian school children in terms of socio-economic grouping and language of origin. Further details of the procedure may be found in the Manual accompanying the Australian Edition of the revised Neale Analysis (Neale 1988).

## Development of the Revised British Edition

The Australian version of the revised Neale Analysis was further changed to take into account relevant aspects of the British educational and cultural environment. Minor modifications were made to the text, to ensure that the language was appropriate to a British audience; for example 'cubby house' was altered to 'tree house'. The balance of male and female characters was altered to minimize any perceived sex role stereotyping. This was achieved by substituting female names and pronouns, and by exchanging some of the main roles. For example, in Form 1 Level 4, the roles of Skipper Kells and Jan were reversed. Such considerations also prompted an exchange of passages between the Diagnostic Tutor and Form 2, so that Form 2 of the British Edition contains one passage at Level 5 which is different from the Australian version.

## Standardization of the Revised British Edition

The British Standardization took place mainly in January and February 1988, early in the second term, when children would already have completed one full term of school. In addition, a number of smaller studies examined other aspects of the test, including the relationship of scores on the Neale Analysis – Revised with those on the original Neale Analysis, and the accuracy with which teachers carried out the scoring procedure. These are discussed in further detail later in this chapter.

### Sample Selection

The standardization sample was drawn to include 400 pupils – 200 boys and 200 girls – from each of the six age groups to which the test applies, i.e. from 6 to 12 years. A total of 317 schools were selected – 62 secondary and 255 primary – from the Department of Education and Science Register of Schools. This register categorizes schools in the following way: type of school ( i.e. maintained or independent, mixed or single sex, infant, middle, secondary etc); age range; number of pupils; and type of county (i.e. metropolitan or non-metropolitan). The sample drawn was representative of the population of schools in England and Wales, in that it accurately reflected the proportion of schools that fall into each of the categories described above. Extra provision was made in drawing up the sample to take account of the expected rate of schools dropping out. (See Table 6.)

**Table 6:** *Numbers of Schools Participating in the British Standardization*

| Age Group | Schools Drawn | Schools Approached | Schools Willing | Schools Making Returns |
|---|---|---|---|---|
| 6:0 – 7:11 | 80 | 80 | 58 | 46 |
| 8:0 – 9:11 | 79 | 75 | 64 | 55 |
| 10:0 – 11:11 | 79 | 79 | 62 | 47 |
| 12 and over | 79 | 76 | 65 | 55 |
| **Total** | **317** | **310** | **256** | **203** |

In the event a total of 1760 children took part in the standardization. A detailed breakdown of this figure is provided in Table 7. The greatest number of schools declining to take part related to the 6 and 7-year-old age groups. In the youngest age group – i.e. 6-year-olds – a total of 195 children were tested on either Form 1 or Form 2, and of the 7-year-olds, a total of 268 pupils took the tests. These numbers are sufficient to provide a satisfactory standardization.

**Table 7:** *Numbers of Children Participating in the British Standardization*

| Age Group | Form 1 | (Boys) | (Girls) | Form 2 | (Boys) | (Girls) | Totals |
|---|---|---|---|---|---|---|---|
| Under 6 | 85 | – | – | 41 | – | – | 126 |
| 6:0 – 6:11 | 118 | (64) | (54) | 77 | (36) | (41) | 195 |
| 7:0 – 7:11 | 165 | (91) | (74) | 103 | (48) | (55) | 268 |
| 8:0 – 8:11 | 149 | (76) | (73) | 129 | (69) | (60) | 278 |
| 9:0 – 9:11 | 136 | (66) | (70) | 108 | (58) | (50) | 244 |
| 10:0 – 10:11 | 130 | (61) | (69) | 126 | (50) | (76) | 256 |
| 11:0 – 11:11 | 142 | (67) | (75) | 120 | (57) | (63) | 262 |
| 12 and over | 73 | – | – | 58 | – | – | 131 |
| **Totals** | **998** | | | **762** | | | **1760** |

Each secondary school was asked to provide six children for testing, and the primary schools were asked to provide twelve children – six from each of two year groups. Schools were asked to select children using a table of random numbers which was sent to them with the test materials. This procedure ensured that all the children in the relevant age groups of the sample had an equal chance of being selected for testing.

## Test Procedure and Materials

A special edition of the Reader, containing Forms 1 and 2, was compiled for standardization. This took the form of a spiral bound booklet similar to the publication edition. The children's performance was recorded in the usual way on a special standardization edition of the Individual Records. Detailed instructions for administering the tests were sent to schools with the test materials. The collation of raw scores and the transformation of these to standardized scores was undertaken by the NFER (National Foundation for Educational Research). The tests were administered either by class teachers or teachers with responsibility for special needs; it was considered advisable that the people adminstering the tests for standardization should as far as possible be those who would administer the tests in schools. The consistency and accuracy with which teachers carried out the testing procedure was the subject of a separate study reported later in this chapter.

Five extra Individual Records were included in the materials sent to each school, so that teachers could gain some experience of the testing procedure before administering the tests for standardization. The option of using these extra Record Forms was taken up by the overwhelming majority of teachers who took part.

Teachers were asked to test children in quiet and familiar surroundings, but within the normal school setting, and, as far as possible, to put children at their ease before testing. Teachers were helped in this latter objective by a new feature of the test – the Practice Passage. The test procedure that the teachers followed was as described on page 12 of this Manual.

To counteract order effects, children were allocated either Form 1 or Form 2 of the test, according to a random number table provided by the NFER. Additional instructions were sent to each school regarding the use of the table of random numbers and the process of selecting children for testing.

## Scoring Procedure

Teachers were asked to record three things: the time taken to read each passage; the number and type of errors made; and the answers children gave to the comprehension questions. This data were used by the NFER to calculate the children's raw scores. Where a basal level was established, full credit was given for the earlier passages that were not actually read – i.e. an accuracy score of 16, and a comprehension score of 4 at level 1 or 8 at level 2 and above. Passages on which the children exceeded the number of permissible errors, or which were attempted but subsequently abandoned, were excluded from the final raw score calculations. A few children in the 6 to 7-year-old age group reached their ceiling on the first passage, and so gained a Raw Score of zero. These children's scores were excluded from the calculation of percentiles and reading ages for Rate, but have been included in the calculations of reading ages for Accuracy and Comprehension.

## Test Reliability

It is possible to report on three main types of reliability measure for the Neale Analysis – Revised: stability (parallel forms) reliability, internal consistency, and standard error of measurement of the test.

### Stability Reliability

Stability reliability is considered by many professionals to be a most important kind of reliability, and is usually determined by the test-retest method. The availability of parallel forms in the Neale Analysis, however, made it possible to report coefficients of stability that are not contaminated by practice on the same test.

During the British Standardization a subsample of children was given both forms of the test: either Form 1, followed after an interval of two days by Form 2, or vice versa. Children were allocated to either procedure on a random basis to counter any order effects which may occur when children gain extra practice by taking one of the tests first. The obtained correlation coefficients between the parallel forms are reported by age group in Table 8.

**Table 8:** *Parallel Form Reliability Coefficients (**r**) for Rate, Accuracy and Comprehension in the Revised British Edition*

*Form 1 followed by Form 2*

|  | Rate | | Accuracy | | Comprehension | |
|---|---|---|---|---|---|---|
| **Age Group** | **r** | **(N)** | **r** | **(N)** | **r** | **(N)** |
| 6:0 –  7:11 | .67 | (33) | .72 | (33) | .89 | (31) |
| 8:0 –  9:11 | .71 | (46) | .94 | (46) | .92 | (46) |
| 10:0 – 11:11 | .95 | (42) | .86 | (42) | .87 | (42) |

*Form 2 followed by Form 1*

|  | Rate | | Accuracy | | Comprehension | |
|---|---|---|---|---|---|---|
| **Age Group** | **r** | **(N)** | **r** | **(N)** | **r** | **(N)** |
| 6:0 –  7:11 | .90 | (19) | .97 | (20) | .96 | (20) |
| 8:0 –  9:11 | .86 | (29) | .98 | (29) | .88 | (29) |
| 10:0 – 11:11 | .89 | (38) | .95 | (38) | .85 | (38) |

**Note. N** = *the number of children on which these statistics are based.*

    One may conclude for the most part that the stability reliability of the Neale Analysis – Revised is high. All of the correlations are statistically reliable above the .001 level of confidence. Yule (1967) noted in relation to the reliability of the original Neale Analysis, 'It can be seen that the Accuracy and Comprehension scales of the reading test are remarkably stable, but. . . the Rate of reading would appear to fluctuate too much to be of much use in individual prediction over a one-year period' (p.225). The lower reliability coefficients for the Rate scores suggest that such scores should be used with some caution.

    One benefit of retaining parallel forms in the Neale Analysis – Revised is that they are useful in follow-up studies or investigations of the effects of teaching upon test performance. The list of references contains a large number of studies in which the Neale Analysis has been utilized in such ways.

### Internal Consistency

The internal consistency of a test estimates the extent to which its items appear to be measuring the same skill. The most common formula for finding the inter-item reliability is that developed by Kuder and Richardson. This is based on the examination of performance on each item and, since it is calculated from the results of a single administration, it provides additional evidence to the stability reliability coefficient derived from test – retest calculations. (See page 49.) However, since the Kuder Richardson formula may only be used with data that is scored either right or wrong, it was considered advisable to use the similar, but more generalized coefficient alpha (Cronbach

1951), which may also be used for continuous data such as the scores calculated for Accuracy. Table 9 shows the internal consistency co-efficients, calculated by using Cronbach's alpha for Accuracy and Comprehension. The procedure for scoring Rate does not enable the calculation of internal consistency coefficients for this score, but stability reliability is reported in Table 8 (See page 50.)

The results for Comprehension, at all age levels, suggest high levels of internal consistency (Guilford, 1965) for both forms. Results for Accuracy suggest somewhat lower levels of reliability, at some age levels, than are usually found with objective reading tests. However, this is probably an outcome of the idiosyncratic prompting and scoring procedures for obtaining Accuracy scores, which do not respond well to conventional internal consistency analysis.

**Table 9:** *Internal Consistency Reliability Coefficients (**r**–Cronbach's Alpha) for Accuracy and Comprehension in the Revised British Edition*

| | ACCURACY | | | | COMPREHENSION | | | |
| --- | --- | --- | --- | --- | --- | --- | --- | --- |
| | Form 1 | | Form 2 | | Form 1 | | Form 2 | |
| Age Group | r | (N) | r | (N) | r | (N) | r | (N) |
| 6:0 – 7:11 | .81 | (283) | .82 | (179) | .91 | (283) | .93 | (179) |
| 8:0 – 9:11 | .87 | (285) | .86 | (237) | .91 | (285) | .91 | (237) |
| 10 and over | .84 | (345) | .85 | (304) | .90 | (345) | .90 | (304) |

**Note. N** = *the number of children on which these statistics are based.*

## Error of Measurement

All educational measurement has some degree of error. We can make estimates of the extent of the errors and use these estimates to describe the range of scores within which the individual would probably score if given the test again. The sources of error stem from the construction of the test and any variations in the procedures used to administer and mark it.

The Standard Error of Measurement is a reflection of the consistency of performance in that it shows the extent of variation due to test error for each score achieved. A 'perfect' test would measure reading ability consistently giving the same result each time the test was administered; there would be no variation in score due to differences in children's vocabulary, motivation or confidence, or due to the procedure used to administer the test or to interpret the answers. Such a test would have zero standard error and total confidence could be placed in the resulting scores, so there would be no need to calculate an equivalent age range. The obtained score would be the 'true' score. However, in practice, test scores do include some error and the Standard Error of Measurement gives an indication of the extent of this error component.

For the Neale Analysis – Revised, the Standard Error of Measurement (SEM) has been calculated using the parallel form reliability co-efficients and the standard deviations of the raw scores for the various components of the test. It varies for each aspect of reading being assessed (Rate, Accuracy, and Comprehension), for each form (1 and 2), and for each age group. These figures are reported in Tables 13 and 14. (See pages 55 and 56.) There, the SEM was calculated using the reliability coefficient for the combined age groups: 6:0−7:11 years; 8:0−9:11 years; 10:0−11:11 years. The standard errors of measurement in raw score units, associated with the three aspects of reading for each form across the entire age range, are reported in Table 10, below.

**Table 10:** *Standard Errors of Measurement in Raw Score Units for All Age Groups Combined in the Revised British Edition*

|          | Rate  | Accuracy | Comprehension |
|----------|-------|----------|---------------|
| **Form 1** | 13.73 | 5.37     | 2.98          |
| **Form 2** | 13.2  | 5.36     | 2.87          |

**Note:** *The Standard Errors of Measurement for each separate age group are reported in Tables 13 (page 55) and 14 (page 56).*

## Test Validity

When evaluating a test, it is most important to know how useful and meaningful are the scores which the test gives: this is essentially what the concept of validity is. A test can be said to be valid if there is evidence available to support inferences drawn from its scores.

Recently, views of validity have emphasized that it is a single concept, related to the test's fitness for its purpose. However, traditionally, the various means of demonstrating a test's validity have been divided into three categories – content-related, criterion-related and construct-related evidence.

### Content Validity

Content validity relates to the extent to which the task content of a test can be said to be a representative sample of the skill or ability the test is designed to measure, and how closely the behaviour demanded by the test resembles 'real-life' activity in that particular area of skill. Clearly the Neale Analysis – Revised requires reading aloud, and the ability to answer comprehension questions. In so far as these are considered important aspects of reading, the test is valid. In contrast, it cannot be considered a valid test of silent reading; if test users consider this latter skill an important one, which they wish to take into account when assessing reading ability, then additional tests should be used. The Neale Analysis – Revised is probably most valid at those stages in the acquisition of reading skills when reading aloud is particularly relevant. To enhance the content validity of the Neale Analysis – Revised at each age group, care was taken during the item development phase to select subject matter for the various reading passages that was suited to the age groups being considered.

### Criterion-Related Validity

Evidence of the *criterion-related validity* of a test comes from its relationship to other assessments purporting to measure the same skill. This kind of validity is often separated into concurrent and predictive aspects: these indicate how well scores on the test relate to performance on similar tests taken at the same time (concurrent) or at a later date (predictive).

Evidence for the *concurrent validity* of the Neale Analysis has been gathered by correlating its subtest scores with scores from other tests which enjoy a wide degree of acceptance as measures of reading or verbal ability.

The original edition of the Neale Analysis (1958) has been correlated with a number of reading scales. It can be seen from Table 11 that the Neale Analysis (1958) Form A produced scores for 9 year olds and 11 year olds which correlate significantly with other standardized measures of reading. Other studies (e.g. Moorhouse & Yule, 1974) have reported similar correlations.

**Table 11:** *Correlations between Rate, Accuracy, and Comprehension for Form A of the Original Neale Analysis, and Criterion Tests of Reading*

|  | *Rate* | | *Accuracy* | | *Comprehension* | |
|---|---|---|---|---|---|---|
|  | **9 year olds** | **11 year olds** | **9 year olds** | **11 year olds** | **9 year olds** | **11 year olds** |
| Ballard One Minute Test | .83 | .80 | .81 | .76 | .65 | .61 |
| Holborn Reading Test (Comprehension) | .74 | .76 | .89 | .88 | .84 | .80 |
| Schonell (Comprehension) | .72 | .81 | .82 | .85 | .79 | .75 |
| Kelvin Reading Test | .65 | .66 | .75 | .78 | .73 | .75 |
| Holborn Reading Test (Accuracy) | .79 | .80 | .94 | .94 | .83 | .76 |
| Vernon Word Reading Test | .78 | .83 | .95 | .94 | .82 | .78 |
| Schonell Word Reading Test | .66 | .79 | .85 | .88 | .80 | .80 |

**Note:** This data is taken from Neale, M.D. (1956). *The construction and standardization of a diagnostic reading test* (pp. 138-139). Unpublished Ph.D. thesis. University of Birmingham, U.K.

Additionally, as part of the Australian 1981-82 standardization of the Revised Neale Analysis, all children who had been tested on the new Australian Edition were also given the Schonell Graded Word Reading Test (Schonell & Goodacre, 1974), and the Vocabulary and Similarities subtests of the WISC-R. Correlations depicting the relationship of these tests with the Revised Neale Analysis (Australian Edition 1988) are presented in Table 12.

**Table 12:** *Correlations between Rate, Accuracy and Comprehension Scores in the Revised Australian Edition, and Criterion Measures of Reading*

|  |  | **WISC-R** | |
|---|---|---|---|
|  | **Schonell** | **Vocabulary** | **Similarities** |
| **Form 2** |  |  |  |
| Rate | .78 | .50 | .47 |
| Accuracy | .96 | .62 | .61 |
| Comprehension | .88 | .68 | .66 |
| (*N*=901) |  |  |  |
| **Form 1** |  |  |  |
| Rate | .76 | .46 | .41 |
| Accuracy | .95 | .58 | .56 |
| Comprehension | .88 | .62 | .60 |
| (*N*=545) |  |  |  |

**Note:** *N=the number of children on which these statistics are based.* **WISC-R**=*the Wechsler Intelligence Scale for Children – Revised.*

The *predictive validity* of the Neale Analysis (1958) has been thoroughly investigated. In a series of studies, Yule (1967, 1973) found that scores obtained from the Neale were an effective way of discriminating between 'backward readers' and 'retarded readers' over a five-year follow-up period. 'Retarded readers' were significantly different from those with 'general' reading backwardness in terms of sex distribution, neurological correlates, and speech and language disorders. McKay (1977), in a four-year follow-up study using results from the Neale Analysis, was able to discriminate effectively between those children who initially were all 'failing to read' and those who, by Grade 4, had become average readers.

With respect to the revised Neale Analysis Australian Edition Form 2, Neale & McKay (1985) found that the Neale test given at the end of Year 1 (rising 6's) correlated significantly on all three scores with reading achievement by the same sample of children tested at the end of Year 2 (rising 7's) (Rate, .73; Accuracy, .83; Comprehension, .78).

## Construct-Related Validity

Evidence for construct-related validity should show that the test score does in fact measure the psychological characteristic of interest – in this case reading ability. For developmental tests, such as the Neale Analysis, increases in score with age may be taken as evidence of construct validity.

The consistent rise in mean scores over the age groups shown in Tables 13 and 14 shows that age differentiation has been achieved for each of the following aspects of reading: Rate, Accuracy and Comprehension. However, Anastasi (1976 p. 166) points out that it is important to remember, in interpreting such age changes, that the test... '*measures behavior characteristics that increase with age under the conditions existing in the type of environment in which the test was standardized*'. In this regard, the characteristics of the standardization sample and their learning environment – i.e. mainstream schools – should be borne in mind. The marked increase in scores from year to year tails off between the ages of 11 and 12, providing an indication of a possible ceiling effect, which suggests that the limits of accuracy and rate of reading have been reached. (See also Tables 15 and 16.)

A further measure of the validity of a diagnostic reading test such as the Neale Analysis is that it can distinguish between groups of children known, or presumed, to have low reading ability, and groups known to possess average reading skills.

There exists a growing collection of studies that have used the Neale Analysis in its original form to investigate differences between different groups of readers such as children from clinics, children with reading problems, children who use different information processing strategies, and children receiving different treatment or educational programmes and from different language backgrounds.

In respect to the first group, Tew and Lawrence (1978), using the Neale Analysis, showed that children with spina bifida attending normal schools were reading at a level that was in line with age expectations, while controls matched for age, sex, social class, etc. in special settings were not. Rutter *et al.* (1980), using the Neale, found in a two-year post-hospitalization follow-up that children who had suffered severe head injuries had more frequent and persistent educational and reading problems than were found in matched controls of children with less severe injuries or orthopaedic injuries. Using the Neale Analysis, Chamberlain, Christie, Holt, Huntley, Pollard, & Roche (1983), in a matched control study, confirmed findings from other studies that virus infections of the central nervous system in infancy may cause severe problems later in school life, including reading difficulties.

**Table 13:** *Form 1, Revised British Edition – Descriptive Statistics in Raw*
*Score Units for Each Age Group*

| Age Groups | 6:0 – 6:11 | 7:0 – 7:11 | 8:0 – 8:11 | 9:0 – 9:11 | 10:0 – 10:11 | 11:0 – 11:11 |
|---|---|---|---|---|---|---|
| **RATE** | | | | | | |
| **Number of Children** | 112 | 165 | 149 | 136 | 129 | 140 |
| **Mean Score** | 41.3 | 52.6 | 66.0 | 73.4 | 83.8 | 90.8 |
| **Standard Deviation of Scores** | 26.5 | 28.5 | 26.8 | 26.1 | 28.3 | 29.2 |
| **ACCURACY** | | | | | | |
| **Number of Children** | 118 | 165 | 149 | 136 | 130 | 142 |
| **Mean Score** | 23.6 | 34.9 | 49.5 | 58.4 | 71.0 | 75.7 |
| **Standard Deviation of Scores** | 17.3 | 18.4 | 21.5 | 21.6 | 20.5 | 19.4 |
| **Maximum Score** | 100 | 100 | 100 | 100 | 100 | 100 |
| **Reliability (Cronbach's Alpha)** | .81 | .81 | .87 | .87 | .84 | .84 |
| **Standard Error of Measurement** | 7.4 | 7.8 | 7.5 | 7.9 | 8.0 | 7.6 |
| **COMPREHENSION** | | | | | | |
| **Number of Children** | 118 | 165 | 149 | 136 | 130 | 142 |
| **Mean Score** | 8.8 | 12.2 | 17.5 | 21.5 | 25.9 | 28.4 |
| **Standard Deviation of Scores** | 6.8 | 6.7 | 8.1 | 8.9 | 8.8 | 8.6 |
| **Maximum Score** | 44 | 44 | 44 | 44 | 44 | 44 |
| **Reliability (Cronbach's Alpha)** | .91 | .91 | .91 | .91 | .91 | .91 |
| **Standard Error of Measurement** | 2.1 | 2.1 | 2.4 | 2.7 | 2.7 | 2.7 |

**Table 14:** *Form 2, Revised British Edition – Descriptive Statistics in Raw Score Units for Each Age Group*

| Age Groups | 6:0 – 6:11 | 7:0 – 7:11 | 8:0 – 8:11 | 9:0 – 9:11 | 10:0 – 10:11 | 11:0 – 11:11 |
|---|---|---|---|---|---|---|
| **RATE** | | | | | | |
| **Number of Children** | 72 | 102 | 129 | 108 | 125 | 120 |
| **Mean Score** | 40.0 | 46.1 | 58.3 | 72.9 | 80.3 | 93.5 |
| **Standard Deviation of Scores** | 23.7 | 23.7 | 27.9 | 29.4 | 25.7 | 33.4 |
| **ACCURACY** | | | | | | |
| **Number of Children** | 77 | 103 | 129 | 108 | 126 | 120 |
| **Mean Score** | 23.0 | 33.6 | 48.3 | 58.7 | 68.8 | 73.6 |
| **Standard Deviation of Scores** | 17.1 | 20.3 | 22.1 | 21.2 | 20.5 | 20.7 |
| **Maximum Score** | 100 | 100 | 100 | 100 | 100 | 100 |
| **Reliability (Cronbach's Alpha)** | .82 | .82 | .86 | .86 | .85 | .85 |
| **Standard Error of Measurement** | 7.2 | 8.5 | 8.2 | 7.8 | 7.7 | 7.7 |
| **COMPREHENSION** | | | | | | |
| **Number of Children** | 77 | 102 | 129 | 108 | 126 | 120 |
| **Mean Score** | 8.6 | 11.7 | 16.7 | 21.2 | 24.1 | 27.1 |
| **Standard Deviation of Scores** | 7.3 | 7.6 | 8.1 | 8.3 | 8.2 | 7.9 |
| **Maximum Score** | 44 | 44 | 44 | 44 | 44 | 44 |
| **Reliability (Cronbach's Alpha)** | .93 | .93 | .91 | .91 | .90 | .90 |
| **Standard Error of Measurement** | 1.8 | 2.1 | 2.4 | 2.4 | 2.5 | 2.5 |

A number of studies have looked at differences between children with reading problems and matched control groups of normal readers. Badcock and Lovegrove (1981) found that children with a lag in mean reading age of four years eight months on the Neale Analysis displayed significant differences in duration of visual persistence when compared with matched controls of normal readers. In a later study, Lovegrove, Martin, Bowling, Blackwood, Badcock, & Paxton (1982) showed that children with a lag of three to four years in mean reading age on the Accuracy scores of the Neale Analysis differed in the pattern of spatial frequencies when compared with matched normal readers.

Poor readers and normal readers of different age groups were matched for reading ability on the Neale Analysis by Bradley & Bryant (1981). They found a strong relationship between reading ability and memory for unfamiliar written words among both groups, but the poor readers had difficulties in detecting rhyme and alliteration. In a somewhat similar study, le Coultre & Carroll (1981), using the Neale Analysis, found differences in reading ability between a group of children trained to read sentences by rhythm and syllable presentation and a similar group using a 'static' whole sentence technique.

Finally, a number of other studies have used the Neale Analysis to show that differences in reading ability are related to visual information store (Lovegrove, Heddle, & Slaghuis, 1980), dark interval threshold perception (Riding & Willetts, 1980), icon persistence (Riding & Pugh, 1977), immigrant and non-immigrant parentage (Yule, Berger, Rutter, & Yule, 1975), parental coaching (Dyson & Swinson, 1982; Bushell, Miller, & Robson, 1982), and antisocial behaviour (Sturge, 1982).

In the original version, a principal component factor analysis was undertaken to determine the independence of the three scores of the Neale Analysis, i.e. Rate, Accuracy, and Comprehension of reading. Two factor analyses were carried out with 200 nine-year-olds and 200 eleven-year-olds. These age groups produced similar factor outcomes with a large general factor accounting for the high intercorrelations. Evidence was obtained, however, of smaller group factors that were interpreted as distinct aspects of reading relating to the mechanical aspects of reading, or decoding and word recognition skills, the understanding of words and ideas, and the rate of reading. While no attempt was made in the restandardization and revision of the Neale Analysis to replicate this factor analytic study, it is reasonable to expect that, since the same structure and items of one form of the original test have been retained, this evidence for the construct validity of the test also applies to the revision. Indeed, in the standardization of the Neale Analysis – Revised intercorrelations between the component scores support such an observation in that they are lower than might be expected if reading were a wholly unitary activity.

**Table 15:** *Intercorrelations Between Component Scores on Form 1 and Form 2 of the Revised British Edition, for All Age Groups Combined*

|  | Rate/ Comprehension | Rate/ Accuracy | Accuracy/ Comprehension |
|---|---|---|---|
| **Form 1 followed by Form 2** | .60 | .70 | .87 |
| **Form 2 followed by Form 1** | .64 | .72 | .88 |

## Sex Differences

In considering the validity of a test, it is important to ensure that the test is an equally valid indicator of performance for both sexes. This may be achieved firstly by ensuring that the test content is of equal interest and relevance to both boys and girls, and secondly by trying to detect and subsequently to remove any biases in performance which become apparent during the construction of the test.

The preparation of the British Edition of the Neale Analysis – Revised included a review of the test content with this issue in mind. Changes from the Australian edition were made with a view to balancing the male and female roles in the test overall; however, it is probably true to say that a very slight male bias still remains. Tables 16 and 17 show the relative performance of boys and girls on each aspect of the test and for each age group. Although there is evidence that the performance of girls is slightly superior to the performance of boys for Rate and Accuracy up to the age of 8:11, this difference tends to disappear in the older age groups. Since the Neale Analysis – Revised is a test of achievement, it was considered important to measure all three aspects of reading, i.e. Rate, Accuracy and Comprehension, although it is known that, in general, boys perform comparatively less well in some of these skill areas.

**Table 16:** *Form 1, Revised British Edition – Mean Raw Scores Achieved by Boys and by Girls in Each Age Group*

|  | Rate | | Accuracy | | Comprehension | |
|---|---|---|---|---|---|---|
| **Age Group** | **Boys** | **Girls** | **Boys** | **Girls** | **Boys** | **Girls** |
| 6:0 – 6:11 | 38 | 46 | 23 | 25 | 9 | 9 |
| 7:0 – 7:11 | 51 | 55 | 34 | 36 | 12 | 12 |
| 8:0 – 8:11 | 62 | 70 | 46 | 53 | 17 | 18 |
| 9:0 – 9:11 | 72 | 74 | 58 | 59 | 22 | 20 |
| 10:0 – 10:11 | 85 | 83 | 73 | 69 | 27 | 25 |
| 11:0 – 11:11 | 88 | 93 | 75 | 76 | 29 | 28 |

**Note:** *All figures have been rounded to the nearest whole number.*

**Table 17:** *Form 2, Revised British Edition – Mean Raw Scores Achieved by Boys and Girls in each Age Group*

|  | Rate | | Accuracy | | Comprehension | |
|---|---|---|---|---|---|---|
| **Age Group** | **Boys** | **Girls** | **Boys** | **Girls** | **Boys** | **Girls** |
| 6:0 – 6:11 | 40 | 40 | 17 | 27 | 6 | 10 |
| 7:0 – 7:11 | 42 | 50 | 32 | 35 | 11 | 12 |
| 8:0 – 8:11 | 53 | 64 | 43 | 54 | 16 | 18 |
| 9:0 – 9:11 | 71 | 75 | 57 | 61 | 21 | 21 |
| 10:0 – 10:11 | 74 | 84 | 67 | 70 | 24 | 23 |
| 11:0 – 11:11 | 87 | 98 | 71 | 76 | 28 | 27 |

**Note:** *All figures have been rounded to the nearest whole number.*

In summary, normal caution should be exercised in accepting any test of a skill as complex as reading. Nevertheless, the foregoing results should give the user confidence that the Neale Analysis of Reading Ability – Revised British Edition, when used with the population for which it was designed, is a valid measure of the Rate, Accuracy, and Comprehension of oral reading ability.

## Comparison between Pupil Performance on the Original Edition, and on the Revised British Edition

At the time of the British standardization, the opportunity was taken to mount a study designed to investigate the relationship between pupils' performance on the two editions of the test. It was considered that this information would be useful to teachers in interpreting scores on the Neale Analysis – Revised, particularly during early use of the test. For this purpose, Form A of the original 1958 edition and Form 1 of the 1989 Revised British Edition were administered to a randomly selected sub-sample of 235 children drawn from the main standardization group. To counter order effects, 117 children took Form 1 first, followed by Form A, and another 118 took Form A first, followed by Form 1. The correlations between scores achieved on the two editions of the test appear in Table 18.

**Table 18:** *Correlations Between Raw Scores on Form A of the Original Neale Analysis, and Form 1 of the Revised British Edition*

|  | Rate | Accuracy | Comprehension |
|---|---|---|---|
| **Form A followed by Form 1** | .82 | .97 | .92 |
| **Form 1 followed by Form A** | .87 | .97 | .92 |

The results on the two forms were also compared using equipercentile equating which involved plotting the raw scores at selected percentiles for Form 1 against those for Form A. For Accuracy and Comprehension the resulting graph showed a linear relationship between the scores achieved on both forms which indicates that the raw scores are more or less equivalent and in fact some raw scores corresponded exactly. It may be assumed therefore that raw scores gained on the Revised British Edition of the test (Form 1) are equivalent to those achieved on the original edition (Form A) for which raw scores were combined in a single table of norms. Thus a raw score of 20 for Comprehension on Form A or B of the 1958 edition is equivalent to a raw score of 20 on Form 1 of the 1989 British Edition.

Scores for rate of reading are more variable by their very nature: while there is a strong relationship between proficiency in reading and rate of reading this is by no means as consistent as that between proficiency in reading and comprehension and accuracy. Rate of reading may also vary with the child's personality or with the style of teaching in the classroom, for example where drama features in the curriculum, oral reading rates may well be lower as children read with more expression. This variability is reflected in the slightly lower correlations for Rate shown in Table 8 and also in Table 17. As there is no shorthand summary for expressing the relationship between scores for Rate on Form 1 of the 1989 Revised British Edition and Form A of the 1958 edition, Table 19 has been provided to help teachers compare scores obtained on the two editions of the test.

The 1988 standardization showed that the earlier norms had become somewhat out of date in the thirty years since they were first collected. The new norms show that children of all ages, but particularly younger children, tend to perform better across the three aspects of reading measured by the Neale Analysis – namely, Rate, Comprehension and Accuracy. For this reason, those schools which have traditionally used certain cut-off points – for example, to screen for children requiring special intervention – will find it best not to rely on specific reading ages, but to use the corresponding raw scores instead. These may be found by consulting the old norms (Neale Analysis of Reading Ability Manual 1958 p.36): find the relevant reading age in the right hand column and read off the corresponding raw score. This raw score value may be used as the cut-off point for Comprehension and Accuracy scores obtained on the Neale Analysis – Revised. For Rate, find the corresponding raw score value for the cut-off point in the same way as described above and consult Table 19 to find the equivalent raw score value for the Neale Analysis – Revised.

**Table 19:** *Rate of Reading – Raw Score Equivalents for Form A of the Original Neale Analysis and Form 1 of the Revised British Edition*

| Form A Score | Form 1 Equivalent Score |
|:---:|:---:|
| 10 | 11 |
| 20 | 16 |
| 30 | 23 |
| 35 | 28 |
| 40 | 34 |
| 45 | 41 |
| 50 | 48 |
| 55 | 54 |
| 60 | 61 |
| 65 | 67 |
| 70 | 74 |
| 75 | 80 |
| 80 | 85 |
| 85 | 89 |
| 90 | 93 |
| 95 | 97 |
| 100 | 103 |
| 110 | 113 |
| 120 | 120 |

## Teacher Accuracy in Carrying out the Test Procedure

It was considered important to involve teachers in the standardization of the Neale Analysis – Revised, as they would be the major users of the test. However, the complexities of administration and of calculating raw scores for Rate, Accuracy and Comprehension were not overlooked. It was decided, therefore, to study this aspect of the test by examining the accuracy with which teachers carried out the testing procedure, obtained scores and transferred these to the front cover of the Individual Record. The children who were included in this study were drawn from the main sample; however, as their data were analysed according to the standardization procedure described on page 47, as well as being scored separately for the Accuracy Study, the results have no implications for the standardization. Nevertheless, conclusions drawn from the study led to modifications of the summary data on the front cover of the Individual Record to include more prominent directions for obtaining raw scores. A total of 79 children and 41 teachers were involved in the Accuracy Study. Tape recordings of the test sessions were made, and the tests were re-scored independently by staff at the NFER. These results were then compared with those obtained by the teachers.

There is some degree of error in all scoring systems particularly where scoring is done by hand rather than by machine. The testing procedure for the Neale Analysis is a complex one, and perfect agreement between scores obtained by teachers and those obtained by NFER staff could not be expected.

Two aspects of the testing procedure were investigated. First, the collection of data – i.e. the reading times recorded, the number or errors and the interpretation of answers to comprehension questions. Incorrect procedures were noted only when they resulted in a Reading Age difference of more than three months. The results below show the percentage of cases for which there is a satisfactory agreement between scores obtained by teachers and scores obtained by NFER staff (i.e. reading ages differed by no more than three months). There was most agreement between these two sets of scores in regard to answers to comprehension questions. The timing of children reading passages was more problematical and there was less agreement here.

| | | |
|---|---|---|
| Comprehension | 84% | ($\pm$ 3 months) |
| Rate | 71% | ($\pm$ 3 months) |
| Accuracy | 75% | ($\pm$ 3 months) |

Taken as a whole these results indicate that most teachers were following the test procedure well.

Secondly, the study examined the transfer of marks to the front cover of the Individual Record. Overall, 11 teachers made transcription errors which would have led to an inaccuracy of greater than three months in the obtained reading age. In general, these errors were either due to miscopying numbers – i.e. 220 for 202 or to overlooking scores on a final passage where it was overleaf. Problems also arose in giving credit for passages below the basal level, and in disregarding scores for passages where the permissible number of errors was exceeded. Additional notes clarifying these procedures are now incorporated on the front page of the Individual Record.

# Answers to Comprehension Questions

## Practice Passages

### Passage X

1 Toys / A box of toys / Playing with toys / Favourite toy / Teddy bear, *etc.*
2 In a box.
3 Teddy bear.
4 Because he is soft/cuddly/furry / Because he stops me feeling frightened/keeps me safe, *or any sensible answer that shows the implied relationship of affinity between the child and a comfort toy.*

### Passage Y

1 Tree-house / Playing in tree-house / Playing space-ships / *or any similar title.*
2 My friend and I / The boy's/girl's friend and him/her.
3 They climbed up a rope.
4 The rope was not there / The rope was pulled up / *or any similar response.*
5 Space-ships.
6 They slid down the rope fast.

## Form 1

### Level 1

*Bird*

1 To my/the window.
2 Bread(crumbs).
3 Built a nest.
4 Looks after/feeds the baby birds/the little ones.

### Level 2

*Road Safety*

1 To school.
2 She saw two children lying on the road / She saw an accident *etc.*
3 They had crashed (into each other).
4 Frightened / Curious / Anxious / Scared / Worried / Upset.
5 She ran to help them.
6 No.
7 Taking part in a lesson / Making a television programme.
8 She saw the cameras / The children pointed to the cameras / The children told her.

## Level 3

*Ali*

1 To shelter.
2 His shoulder bumped/knocked against it.
3 He fell into an underground room/cellar.
4 Precious jewels.
5 He did not think that they were real / He thought his eyes were playing tricks on him / He thought he was imagining things.
6 A way to escape / A way out.
7 To find that the jewels were real / The jewels were still there.
8 They belonged to a buried palace of long ago.

## Level 4

*Jan*

1 *Two of:* Diving belt / Weights / Air-hose.
2 He supervised her air-hose / He stopped the air-hose from tangling.
3 By following the bubbles.
4 Specimens and/or crayfish.
5 It advanced/swam directly towards her.
6 She retreated cautiously and remained motionless / She kept still *etc.*
7 Rocky grooves.
8 She wanted to protect her baby sharks / She was worried about the baby sharks *etc.*

## Level 5

*The Fox*

1 Mankind / People / Humans.
2 To divert/break its scent trail, *or any similar response.*
3 Both parents / The parents.
4 From their hunting expeditions / Knowledge of the area.
5 To a mine-shaft / A neglected mine-shaft / An old mine.
6 No / It had been closed down.
7 It skirted the hedge / It went round the hedge / It pretended to jump over.
8 Because the hedge enclosed the mine-shaft / Because the hedge was in the way / Because they were intent on the fox.

## Level 6

*Migration*

1 In Spring.
2 Because they migrate / The distances birds fly / Regular journeys of the birds, *or any similar answer.*
3 Many birds migrate in summer / Many birds stay in winter.
4 It doesn't seem so / No / They generally fly or migrate alone.
5 It's inborn / Inborn behaviour / Instinct, *etc.*
6 Germany.
7 South-easterly / Easterly.
8 South-easterly / Easterly / Same way.

# Form 2

## Level 1

### Kitten

1 A (black) cat / A kitten.
2 By the door.
3 She went away.
4 Kept it (for a pet).

## Level 2

### Surprise Parcel

1 Saturday.
2 It was a surprise parcel / It says it was a surprise.
3 Jane.
4 It had strange stamps.
5 Their uncle.
6 Skates.
7 An electric train.
8 They had wanted these things for a long time.

## Level 3

### Circus

1 Circus / Tent / Big top / Circus ring.
2 The end.
3 To clear the ring / To take the lions away.
4 Thunder had frightened them / Because of the thunder.
5 She stumbled/fell over / She lost her whip / A lion jumped at her.
6 He cracked the whip / He saved Tina / He controlled the lions.
7 Tina.
8 That he would be a lion tamer / On his future work...(*explanation required*).

## Level 4

### Dragon

1 By the roaring of the dragon.
2 Marsh land *or similar response*.
3 By whipping its tail around the horse's legs.
4 When the dragon was off-guard/wasn't looking.
5 That he was wounded/hurt/dead.
6 He was used to quick victories / He was very powerful.
7 Under the wing.
8 Because they would not be troubled again (by the dragon).

## Level 5

### Brigantine

1 The voyage of Sir Francis Drake.
2 *Both of:* To carry out scientific projects **and** provide community services.

**3** Selected from different nations / Selected for their enthusiasm and different abilities.

**4** Because the voyage had outstripped their dreams / They did more than they had expected, etc.

**5** They were supervised by scientists / Scientists helped them.

**6** *Any two of:* They salvaged ancient wrecks / They rebuilt houses / They mapped jungle trails / They studied forests / They did relief work.

**7** They had to overcome disabilities.

**8** Courage and adaptability *and* a spirit of adventure.

## Level 6

*Everest*

**1** Rest.

**2** Pitch (an intermediate) camp.

**3** They were pleased/relieved.

**4** A rescue from a crevasse / One of the team had fallen into a crevasse.

**5** Violent/incessant winds.

**6** A steep rise / A slope.

**7** The tracks of the advance party had disappeared.

**8** It had not been conquered before / They would be the first to reach it.

# Diagnostic Tutor

## Level 1

*The Box*

**1** Mother.

**2** On the table.

**3** A toy. *Accept any toy that the child might name.*

**4** A white rabbit.

## Level 1

*Lost and Found*

**1** The wind blew it out to sea / The wind blew it away.

**2** He went for it / He got it / He brought it back.

**3** Yes.

**4** It became a little boy's/girl's pet / It went to live with the little boy/girl / It had been lost and then he/she gave it a home.

## Level 2

*Fisherman*

**1** Looking for tadpoles.

**2** A splash.

**3** A fisherman had fallen into the lake.

**4** Because he was hurt.

**5** They tried to pull him ashore.

**6** He was too heavy.

**7** She held the man's head above water.
**8** He ran/raced for help.

## Level 2

*Helicopter*

**1** The dog's barking woke them up / The noise of the helicopter crashing.
**2** They ran to the window / They looked out of the window.
**3** Flashing lights and smoke.
**4** A helicopter had crash-landed.
**5** In the park nearby.
**6** Ambulance / Fire brigade / Lights on helicopter / Emergency lights, *etc.*
**7** A fire had broken out / Flames were shooting up / There might be an explosion, *etc.*
**8** He jumped out/ran clear, *etc.*

## Level 3

*Seagull*

**1** The thud/noise of the seagull landing / They noticed the stillness of the gull.
**2** Its wings were covered in oil / stuck like glue, *etc.*
**3** A tanker had been damaged and oil had leaked into the sea.
**4** To explore / To explore the rock pools.
**5** It looked dead / It was very still *or any similar answer.*
**6** It cheeped feebly / It made a noise.
**7** They wrapped it in Nick's shirt and went for help / It was taken to the zoo.
**8** Yes. *(Q. How do you know?)* Because it returned safely to sea.

## Level 3

*Penguins*

**1** The penguins / The penguin parade, *etc.*
**2** At dusk / In the evening.
**3** There was no sign of life (on the sand-hills or on the beach).
**4** Because of the floodlights/the lights.
**5** They staggered up the path, weighed down with fish / It was hilly on the way to the burrows.
**6** In the sand-hills.
**7** The paths were well-worn.
**8** Because they thrust their heads out impatiently / Because they were waiting for the fish from their parents, *or any sensible answer.*

## Level 4

*Ghosts*

**1** Dark clouds blotted out the daylight / Because of the dark clouds / It got darker.
**2** Explore.
**3** Mournful wailing / They were afraid of the noise / They thought they heard ghosts.
**4** They went cautiously towards the noise / They went to find out what it was.

**5** The old kitchen.
**6** An exhausted dog / That a dog had been trapped in there.
**7** He had been hunting for rats.
**8** He was exhausted/frightened, and couldn't get out.

## Level 5

*Submarine*

**1** To rescue the men in the submarine.
**2** Thirty metres.
**3** Treacherous currents.
**4** Disciplined / Confident / Calm.
**5** His lifeline caught/entangled on the wreckage.
**6** Not to jerk the line free by force / Not to use force.
**7** He kept calm / He was patient / He showed persistence/courage.
**8** He rescued the people in the submarine / He carried on with the rescue work.

## Level 6

*Volcano*

**1** To record the activity of the volcano / To photograph the volcano and make records, *etc.*
**2** It had been dormant/inactive/quiet *etc.* for a long time but now had begun smouldering.
**3** Loud rumbling / A loud noise.
**4** Near the crater's edge / Near the top of the volcano.
**5** The rocks fell on the opposite slope.
**6** They threw away/abandoned their equipment.
**7** One person was struck by a rock/boulder, *etc.*
**8** Because their surroundings were about to be destroyed *or similar response.*

## Extension Level

*Coto Doñana*

**1** *Any of the following:* The importance of nature / The relationship of all life to environment / The significance of conservation of nature / The wildlife of Coto Doñana / The Spanish sanctuary for conservation.
**2** Their adaptability.
**3** Combination of climate, isolation and physical natural conditions / It is on the migration route for birds.
**4** The Spanish government and the World Wildlife Fund.
**5** It provides suitable places for these species to live, *or any similar suitable answer.*
**6** Hunting.
**7** The importance of conservation / Inter-dependence of all forms of life / We must prize/protect **all** flora and fauna.
**8** *Accept any well known issue concerning conservation in the world, e.g.* Whales / Baby seals / Pollution of waterways / Nuclear waste disposal / Great Barrier Reef.

# Conversion Tables

**Note:** *The conversion tables for Form 2 have been shaded to help users identify the tables which relate to the standardized form they have been using.*

# Reading Age: ACCURACY

e: row of extrapolated scores

| | Raw Score | Reading Age (Yrs : Mths) | Equivalent Age Range (Yrs : Mths) | | Raw Score | Reading Age (Yrs : Mths) | Equivalent Age Range (Yrs : Mths) |
|---|---|---|---|---|---|---|---|
| | **FORM 1** | | | | **FORM 2** | | |
| | * * * | * * * | * * * | | * * * | * * * | * * * |
| | * * * | * * * | * * * | | * * * | * * * | * * * |
| | * * * | * * * | * * * | | * * * | * * * | * * * |
| | * * * | * * * | * * * | | * * * | * * * | * * * |
| | * * * | * * * | * * * | | * * * | * * * | * * * |
| | * * * | * * * | * * * | | * * * | * * * | * * * |
| e | 7 | 5:00 | 3:07 to 6:05 | e | 7 | 5:00 | 3:08 to 6:04 |
| e | 8 | 5:01 | 3:08 to 6:06 | e | 8 | 5:01 | 3:09 to 6:05 |
| e | 9 | 5:02 | 3:09 to 6:07 | e | 9 | 5:02 | 3:10 to 6:06 |
| e | 10 | 5:03 | 3:10 to 6:08 | e | 10 | 5:03 | 3:11 to 6:07 |
| e | 11 | 5:04 | 3:11 to 6:09 | e | 11 | 5:04 | 4:00 to 6:08 |
| e | 12 | 5:05 | 4:00 to 6:10 | e | 12 | 5:05 | 4:01 to 6:09 |
| e | 13 | 5:06 | 4:01 to 6:10 | e | 13 | 5:06 | 4:02 to 6:10 |
| e | 14 | 5:07 | 4:02 to 6:11 | e | 14 | 5:07 | 4:03 to 6:11 |
| e | 15 | 5:08 | 4:03 to 7:00 | e | 15 | 5:08 | 4:04 to 7:00 |
| e | 16 | 5:09 | 4:04 to 7:01 | e | 16 | 5:09 | 4:05 to 7:01 |
| e | 17 | 5:10 | 4:05 to 7:02 | e | 17 | 5:10 | 4:06 to 7:02 |
| e | 18 | 5:11 | 4:06 to 7:03 | e | 18 | 5:11 | 4:07 to 7:03 |
| e | 19 | 6:00 | 4:07 to 7:04 | | 19 | 6:00 | 4:08 to 7:04 |
| | 20 | 6:00 | 4:07 to 7:05 | | 20 | 6:01 | 4:09 to 7:05 |
| | 21 | 6:01 | 4:08 to 7:06 | | 21 | 6:02 | 4:10 to 7:06 |
| | 22 | 6:02 | 4:09 to 7:07 | | 22 | 6:03 | 4:11 to 7:07 |
| | 23 | 6:03 | 4:10 to 7:08 | | 23 | 6:04 | 5:00 to 7:08 |
| | 24 | 6:04 | 4:11 to 7:08 | | 24 | 6:05 | 5:01 to 7:09 |
| | 25 | 6:05 | 5:00 to 7:10 | | 25 | 6:06 | 5:02 to 7:10 |
| | 26 | 6:06 | 5:01 to 7:11 | | 26 | 6:07 | 5:03 to 7:11 |
| | 27 | 6:07 | 5:02 to 8:00 | | 27 | 6:08 | 5:04 to 8:00 |
| | 28 | 6:08 | 5:03 to 8:01 | | 28 | 6:09 | 5:05 to 8:01 |
| | 29 | 6:09 | 5:04 to 8:02 | | 29 | 6:10 | 5:06 to 8:02 |
| | 30 | 6:10 | 5:05 to 8:03 | | 30 | 6:11 | 5:07 to 8:03 |
| | 31 | 6:11 | 5:06 to 8:04 | | 31 | 7:00 | 5:08 to 8:04 |
| | 32 | 7:00 | 5:07 to 8:05 | | 32 | 7:01 | 5:09 to 8:05 |
| | 33 | 7:02 | 5:09 to 8:07 | | 33 | 7:02 | 5:10 to 8:06 |
| | 34 | 7:03 | 5:10 to 8:08 | | 34 | 7:03 | 5:11 to 8:07 |
| | 35 | 7:04 | 5:11 to 8:07 | | 35 | 7:04 | 6:00 to 8:08 |
| | 36 | 7:05 | 6:00 to 8:10 | | 36 | 7:05 | 6:01 to 8:09 |
| | 37 | 7:06 | 6:01 to 8:11 | | 37 | 7:06 | 6:02 to 8:10 |
| | 38 | 7:07 | 6:02 to 9:00 | | 38 | 7:08 | 6:04 to 9:00 |
| | 39 | 7:08 | 6:03 to 9:01 | | 39 | 7:09 | 6:05 to 9:01 |
| | 40 | 7:09 | 6:04 to 9:02 | | 40 | 7:10 | 6:06 to 9:02 |
| | 41 | 7:10 | 6:05 to 9:03 | | 41 | 7:11 | 6:07 to 9:03 |
| | 42 | 7:11 | 6:06 to 9:04 | | 42 | 8:00 | 6:08 to 9:04 |
| | 43 | 8:01 | 6:08 to 9:06 | | 43 | 8:01 | 6:09 to 9:05 |
| | 44 | 8:02 | 6:09 to 9:07 | | 44 | 8:02 | 6:10 to 9:06 |
| | 45 | 8:03 | 6:10 to 9:08 | | 45 | 8:04 | 7:00 to 9:08 |
| | 46 | 8:04 | 6:11 to 9:09 | | 46 | 8:05 | 7:01 to 9:09 |
| | 47 | 8:05 | 7:00 to 9:10 | | 47 | 8:06 | 7:02 to 9:10 |
| | 48 | 8:06 | 7:01 to 9:11 | | 48 | 8:07 | 7:03 to 9:11 |
| | 49 | 8:07 | 7:02 to 10:00 | | 49 | 8:08 | 7:04 to 10:00 |
| | 50 | 8:09 | 7:04 to 10:02 | | 50 | 8:09 | 7:05 to 10:01 |

continued on next page

# Reading Age: ACCURACY

e: row of extrapolated scores

| | FORM 1 | | | | FORM 2 | |
|---|---|---|---|---|---|---|
| Raw Score | Reading Age (Yrs : Mths) | Equivalent Age Range (Yrs : Mths) | | Raw Score | Reading Age (Yrs : Mths) | Equivalent Age Range (Yrs : Mths) |
| 51 | 8:10 | 7:05 to 10:03 | | 51 | 8:11 | 7:07 to 10:03 |
| 52 | 8:11 | 7:06 to 10:04 | | 52 | 9:00 | 7:08 to 10:04 |
| 53 | 9:00 | 7:07 to 10:05 | | 53 | 9:01 | 7:09 to 10:05 |
| 54 | 9:01 | 7:08 to 10:06 | | 54 | 9:02 | 7:10 to 10:06 |
| 55 | 9:03 | 7:10 to 10:08 | | 55 | 9:04 | 8:00 to 10:08 |
| 56 | 9:04 | 7:11 to 10:09 | | 56 | 9:05 | 8:01 to 10:09 |
| 57 | 9:05 | 8:00 to 10:10 | | 57 | 9:06 | 8:02 to 10:10 |
| 58 | 9:06 | 8:01 to 10:11 | | 58 | 9:07 | 8:03 to 10:11 |
| 59 | 9:08 | 8:03 to 11:01 | | 59 | 9:08 | 8:04 to 11:00 |
| 60 | 9:09 | 8:04 to 11:02 | | 60 | 9:10 | 8:06 to 11:02 |
| 61 | 9:10 | 8:05 to 11:03 | | 61 | 9:11 | 8:07 to 11:03 |
| 62 | 9:11 | 8:06 to 11:04 | | 62 | 10:00 | 8:08 to 11:04 |
| 63 | 10:01 | 8:08 to 11:06 | | 63 | 10:02 | 8:10 to 11:06 |
| 64 | 10:02 | 8:09 to 11:07 | | 64 | 10:03 | 8:11 to 11:07 |
| 65 | 10:03 | 8:10 to 11:08 | | 65 | 10:04 | 9:00 to 11:08 |
| 66 | 10:04 | 8:11 to 11:09 | | 66 | 10:05 | 9:01 to 11:09 |
| 67 | 10:06 | 9:01 to 11:11 | | 67 | 10:07 | 9:03 to 11:11 |
| 68 | 10:07 | 9:02 to 12:00 | | 68 | 10:08 | 9:04 to 12:00 |
| 69 | 10:08 | 9:03 to 12:01 | | 69 | 10:09 | 9:05 to 12:01 |
| 70 | 10:10 | 9:05 to 12:03 | | 70 | 10:11 | 9:07 to 12:03 |
| 71 | 10:11 | 9:06 to 12:04 | | 71 | 11:00 | 9:08 to 12:04 |
| 72 | 11:00 | 9:07 to 12:05 | | 72 | 11:01 | 9:09 to 12:05 |
| 73 | 11:02 | 9:09 to 12:07 | | 73 | 11:03 | 9:11 to 12:07 |
| 74 | 11:03 | 9:10 to 12:08 | | 74 | 11:04 | 10:00 to 12:08 |
| 75 | 11:04 | 9:11 to 12:09 | | 75 | 11:05 | 10:01 to 12:09 |
| 76 | 11:06 | 10:01 to 12:11 | | 76 | 11:07 | 10:03 to 12:11 |
| 77 | 11:07 | 10:02 to 13:00 | | 77 | 11:08 | 10:04 to 13:00 |
| 78 | 11:08 | 10:03 to 13:01 | | 78 | 11:10 | 10:06 to 13:02 |
| 79 | 11:10 | 10:05 to 13:03 | | 79 | 11:11 | 10:07 to 13:03 |
| 80 | 11:11 | 10:06 to 13:04 | e 80 | 12:00 | 10:08 to 13:04 |
| e 81 | 12:01 | 10:08 to 13:06 | e 81 | 12:02 | 10:10 to 13:06 |
| e 82 | 12:02 | 10:09 to 13:07 | e 82 | 12:03 | 10:11 to 13:07 |
| e 83 | 12:03 | 10:10 to 13:08 | e 83 | 12:05 | 11:01 to 13:09 |
| e 84 | 12:05 | 11:00 to 13:10 | e 84 | 12:06 | 11:02 to 13:10 |
| e 85 | 12:06 | 11:01 to 13:11 | e 85 | 12:07 | 11:03 to 13:11 |
| e 86 | 12:08 | 11:03 to 14:01 | e 86 | 12:09 | 11:05 to 14:01 |
| e 87 | 12:09 | 11:04 to 14:02 | e 87 | 12:10 | 11:06 to 14:02 |
| e 88 | 12:10 | 11:05 to 14:03 | e 88 | 13:00 | 11:08 to 14:04 |
| e 89 | 13:00 | 11:07 to 14:05 | 89 to 100 | 13:00 + | 11:09 + |
| 90 to 100 | 13:00 + | 11:08 + | *** | *** | *** |

# Reading Age: RATE

e: row of extrapolated scores

| | FORM 1 | | | | FORM 2 | | |
|---|---|---|---|---|---|---|---|
| | Raw Score | Reading Age (Yrs : Mths) | Equivalent Age Range (Yrs : Mths) | | Raw Score | Reading Age (Yrs : Mths) | Equivalent Age Range (Yrs : Mths) |
| | *** | *** | *** | e | 21 | 5:01 | 3:07 to 6:07 |
| e | 22 | 5:00 | 3:05 to 6:07 | e | 22 | 5:02 | 3:08 to 6:08 |
| e | 23 | 5:01 | 3:06 to 6:08 | e | 23 | 5:03 | 3:09 to 6:09 |
| e | 24 | 5:01 | 3:06 to 6:08 | e | 24 | 5:04 | 3:10 to 6:10 |
| e | 25 | 5:02 | 3:07 to 6:09 | e | 25 | 5:05 | 3:11 to 6:11 |
| e | 26 | 5:03 | 3:08 to 6:10 | e | 26 | 5:06 | 4:00 to 7:00 |
| e | 27 | 5:04 | 3:09 to 6:11 | e | 27 | 5:07 | 4:01 to 7:01 |
| e | 28 | 5:05 | 3:10 to 7:00 | e | 28 | 5:09 | 4:03 to 7:03 |
| e | 29 | 5:06 | 3:11 to 7:01 | e | 29 | 5:10 | 4:04 to 7:04 |
| e | 30 | 5:07 | 4:00 to 7:02 | e | 30 | 5:11 | 4:05 to 7:05 |
| e | 31 | 5:08 | 4:01 to 7:03 | | 31 | 6:00 | 4:06 to 7:06 |
| e | 32 | 5:09 | 4:02 to 7:04 | | 32 | 6:01 | 4:07 to 7:07 |
| e | 33 | 5:10 | 4:03 to 7:05 | | 33 | 6:02 | 4:08 to 7:08 |
| e | 34 | 5:11 | 4:04 to 7:06 | | 34 | 6:03 | 4:09 to 7:09 |
| | 35 | 6:00 | 4:05 to 7:07 | | 35 | 6:04 | 4:10 to 7:10 |
| | 36 | 6:01 | 4:06 to 7:08 | | 36 | 6:05 | 4:11 to 7:11 |
| | 37 | 6:01 | 4:06 to 7:08 | | 37 | 6:06 | 5:00 to 8:00 |
| | 38 | 6:02 | 4:07 to 7:09 | | 38 | 6:07 | 5:01 to 8:01 |
| | 39 | 6:03 | 4:08 to 7:10 | | 39 | 6:08 | 5:02 to 8:02 |
| | 40 | 6:04 | 4:09 to 7:11 | | 40 | 6:09 | 5:03 to 8:03 |
| | 41 | 6:05 | 4:10 to 8:00 | | 41 | 6:10 | 5:04 to 8:04 |
| | 42 | 6:06 | 4:11 to 8:01 | | 42 | 6:11 | 5:05 to 8:05 |
| | 43 | 6:07 | 5:00 to 8:02 | | 43 | 7:00 | 5:06 to 8:06 |
| | 44 | 6:08 | 5:01 to 8:03 | | 44 | 7:01 | 5:07 to 8:07 |
| | 45 | 6:09 | 5:02 to 8:04 | | 45 | 7:02 | 5:08 to 8:08 |
| | 46 | 6:10 | 5:03 to 8:05 | | 46 | 7:04 | 5:10 to 8:10 |
| | 47 | 6:11 | 5:04 to 8:06 | | 47 | 7:05 | 5:11 to 8:11 |
| | 48 | 7:01 | 5:06 to 8:08 | | 48 | 7:06 | 6:00 to 9:00 |
| | 49 | 7:02 | 5:07 to 8:09 | | 49 | 7:07 | 6:01 to 9:01 |
| | 50 | 7:03 | 5:08 to 8:10 | | 50 | 7:08 | 6:02 to 9:02 |
| | 51 | 7:04 | 5:09 to 8:11 | | 51 | 7:09 | 6:03 to 9:03 |
| | 52 | 7:05 | 5:10 to 9:00 | | 52 | 7:10 | 6:04 to 9:04 |
| | 53 | 7:06 | 5:11 to 9:01 | | 53 | 7:11 | 6:05 to 9:05 |
| | 54 | 7:07 | 6:00 to 9:02 | | 54 | 8:00 | 6:06 to 9:06 |
| | 55 | 7:08 | 6:01 to 9:03 | | 55 | 8:01 | 6:07 to 9:07 |
| | 56 | 7:09 | 6:02 to 9:04 | | 56 | 8:02 | 6:08 to 9:08 |
| | 57 | 7:10 | 6:03 to 9:05 | | 57 | 8:03 | 6:09 to 9:09 |
| | 58 | 7:11 | 6:04 to 9:06 | | 58 | 8:04 | 6:10 to 9:10 |
| | 59 | 8:00 | 6:05 to 9:07 | | 59 | 8:05 | 6:11 to 9:11 |
| | 60 | 8:01 | 6:06 to 9:08 | | 60 | 8:06 | 7:00 to 10:00 |
| | 61 | 8:03 | 6:08 to 9:10 | | 61 | 8:07 | 7:01 to 10:01 |
| | 62 | 8:04 | 6:09 to 9:11 | | 62 | 8:08 | 7:02 to 10:02 |
| | 63 | 8:05 | 6:10 to 10:00 | | 63 | 8:09 | 7:03 to 10:03 |
| | 64 | 8:06 | 6:11 to 10:01 | | 64 | 8:11 | 7:05 to 10:05 |
| | 65 | 8:07 | 7:00 to 10:02 | | 65 | 9:00 | 7:06 to 10:06 |
| | 66 | 8:08 | 7:01 to 10:03 | | 66 | 9:01 | 7:07 to 10:07 |
| | 67 | 8:09 | 7:02 to 10:04 | | 67 | 9:02 | 7:08 to 10:08 |
| | 68 | 8:11 | 7:04 to 10:06 | | 68 | 9:03 | 7:09 to 10:09 |
| | 69 | 9:00 | 7:05 to 10:07 | | 69 | 9:04 | 7:10 to 10:10 |
| | 70 | 9:01 | 7:06 to 10:08 | | 70 | 9:05 | 7:11 to 10:11 |

continued on next page

# Reading Age: RATE

e: row of extrapolated scores

| | FORM 1 | | | | FORM 2 | | |
|---|---|---|---|---|---|---|---|
| | Raw Score | Reading Age (Yrs : Mths) | Equivalent Age Range (Yrs : Mths) | | Raw Score | Reading Age (Yrs : Mths) | Equivalent Age Range (Yrs : Mths) |
| | 71 | 9:02 | 7:07 to 10:09 | | 71 | 9:06 | 8:00 to 11:00 |
| | 72 | 9:03 | 7:08 to 10:10 | | 72 | 9:07 | 8:01 to 11:01 |
| | 73 | 9:05 | 7:10 to 11:00 | | 73 | 9:08 | 8:02 to 11:02 |
| | 74 | 9:06 | 7:11 to 11:01 | | 74 | 9:09 | 8:03 to 11:03 |
| | 75 | 9:07 | 8:00 to 11:02 | | 75 | 9:10 | 8:04 to 11:04 |
| | 76 | 9:08 | 8:01 to 11:03 | | 76 | 9:11 | 8:05 to 11:05 |
| | 77 | 9:09 | 8:02 to 11:04 | | 77 | 10:00 | 8:06 to 11:06 |
| | 78 | 9:11 | 8:04 to 11:06 | | 78 | 10:01 | 8:07 to 11:07 |
| | 79 | 10:00 | 8:05 to 11:07 | | 79 | 10:02 | 8:08 to 11:08 |
| | 80 | 10:01 | 8:06 to 11:08 | | 80 | 10:03 | 8:09 to 11:09 |
| | 81 | 10:02 | 8:07 to 11:09 | | 81 | 10:04 | 8:10 to 11:10 |
| | 82 | 10:04 | 8:09 to 11:11 | | 82 | 10:06 | 9:00 to 12:00 |
| | 83 | 10:05 | 8:10 to 12:00 | | 83 | 10:07 | 9:01 to 12:01 |
| | 84 | 10:06 | 8:11 to 12:01 | | 84 | 10:08 | 9:02 to 12:02 |
| | 85 | 10:07 | 9:00 to 12:02 | | 85 | 10:09 | 9:03 to 12:03 |
| | 86 | 10:09 | 9:02 to 12:04 | | 86 | 10:10 | 9:04 to 12:04 |
| | 87 | 10:10 | 9:03 to 12:05 | | 87 | 10:11 | 9:05 to 12:05 |
| | 88 | 10:11 | 9:04 to 12:06 | | 88 | 11:00 | 9:06 to 12:06 |
| | 89 | 11:01 | 9:06 to 12:08 | | 89 | 11:01 | 9:07 to 12:07 |
| | 90 | 11:02 | 9:07 to 12:09 | | 90 | 11:02 | 9:08 to 12:08 |
| | 91 | 11:03 | 9:08 to 12:10 | | 91 | 11:03 | 9:09 to 12:09 |
| | 92 | 11:05 | 9:10 to 13:00 | | 92 | 11:04 | 9:10 to 12:10 |
| | 93 | 11:06 | 9:11 to 13:01 | | 93 | 11:05 | 9:11 to 12:11 |
| | 94 | 11:07 | 10:00 to 13:02 | | 94 | 11:06 | 10:00 to 13:00 |
| | 95 | 11:09 | 10:02 to 13:04 | | 95 | 11:07 | 10:01 to 13:01 |
| | 96 | 11:10 | 10:03 to 13:05 | | 96 | 11:08 | 10:02 to 13:02 |
| | 97 | 11:11 | 10:04 to 13:06 | | 97 | 11:09 | 10:03 to 13:03 |
| e | 98 | 12:01 | 10:06 to 13:08 | | 98 | 11:10 | 10:04 to 13:04 |
| e | 99 | 12:02 | 10:07 to 13:09 | | 99 | 11:11 | 10:05 to 13:05 |
| e | 100 | 12:03 | 10:08 to 13:10 | e | 100 | 12:01 | 10:07 to 13:07 |
| e | 101 | 12:05 | 10:10 to 14:00 | e | 101 | 12:02 | 10:08 to 13:08 |
| e | 102 | 12:06 | 10:11 to 14:01 | e | 102 | 12:03 | 10:09 to 13:09 |
| e | 103 | 12:07 | 11:00 to 14:02 | e | 103 | 12:04 | 10:10 to 13:10 |
| e | 104 | 12:09 | 11:02 to 14:04 | e | 104 | 12:05 | 10:11 to 13:11 |
| e | 105 | 12:10 | 11:03 to 14:05 | e | 105 | 12:06 | 11:00 to 14:00 |
| e | 106 | 13:00 | 11:05 to 14:07 | e | 106 | 12:07 | 11:01 to 14:01 |
| | 107 + | 13:00 + | 11:06 + | e | 107 | 12:08 | 11:02 to 14:02 |
| | *** | *** | *** | e | 108 | 12:09 | 11:03 to 14:03 |
| | *** | *** | *** | e | 109 | 12:10 | 11:04 to 14:04 |
| | *** | *** | *** | e | 110 | 12:11 | 11:05 to 14:05 |
| | *** | *** | *** | e | 111 | 13:00 | 11:06 to 14:06 |
| | *** | *** | *** | | 112 + | 13:00 + | 11:07 + |
| | *** | *** | *** | | *** | *** | *** |
| | *** | *** | *** | | *** | *** | *** |
| | *** | *** | *** | | *** | *** | *** |
| | *** | *** | *** | | *** | *** | *** |
| | *** | *** | *** | | *** | *** | *** |
| | *** | *** | *** | | *** | *** | *** |
| | *** | *** | *** | | *** | *** | *** |
| | *** | *** | *** | | *** | *** | *** |

# Reading Age: COMPREHENSION

e: row of extrapolated scores

| | | FORM 1 | | | | FORM 2 | |
|---|---|---|---|---|---|---|---|
| | Raw Score | Reading Age (Yrs : Mths) | Equivalent Age Range (Yrs : Mths) | | Raw Score | Reading Age (Yrs : Mths) | Equivalent Age Range (Yrs : Mths) |
| | *** | *** | *** | | *** | *** | *** |
| e | 2 | 5:01 | 3:08 to 6:06 | e | 2 | 5:00 | 3:07 to 6:05 |
| e | 3 | 5:03 | 3:10 to 6:08 | e | 3 | 5:03 | 3:10 to 6:08 |
| e | 4 | 5:06 | 4:01 to 6:11 | e | 4 | 5:05 | 4:00 to 6:10 |
| e | 5 | 5:08 | 4:03 to 7:01 | e | 5 | 5:08 | 4:03 to 7:01 |
| e | 6 | 5:10 | 4:05 to 7:03 | | 6 | 5:10 | 4:05 to 7:03 |
| | 7 | 6:01 | 4:08 to 7:06 | | 7 | 6:01 | 4:08 to 7:06 |
| | 8 | 6:04 | 4:11 to 7:09 | | 8 | 6:04 | 4:11 to 7:09 |
| | 9 | 6:06 | 5:01 to 7:11 | | 9 | 6:07 | 5:02 to 8:00 |
| | 10 | 6:09 | 5:04 to 8:02 | | 10 | 6:09 | 5:04 to 8:02 |
| | 11 | 6:11 | 5:06 to 8:04 | | 11 | 7:00 | 5:07 to 8:05 |
| | 12 | 7:02 | 5:09 to 8:07 | | 12 | 7:03 | 5:10 to 8:08 |
| | 13 | 7:05 | 6:00 to 8:10 | | 13 | 7:06 | 6:01 to 8:11 |
| | 14 | 7:08 | 6:03 to 9:01 | | 14 | 7:09 | 6:04 to 9:02 |
| | 15 | 7:11 | 6:06 to 9:04 | | 15 | 8:00 | 6:07 to 9:05 |
| | 16 | 8:02 | 6:09 to 9:07 | | 16 | 8:03 | 6:10 to 9:08 |
| | 17 | 8:05 | 7:00 to 9:10 | | 17 | 8:07 | 7:02 to 10:00 |
| | 18 | 8:08 | 7:03 to 10:01 | | 18 | 8:10 | 7:05 to 10:03 |
| | 19 | 8:11 | 7:06 to 10:04 | | 19 | 9:01 | 7:08 to 10:06 |
| | 20 | 9:02 | 7:09 to 10:07 | | 20 | 9:05 | 8:00 to 10:10 |
| | 21 | 9:05 | 8:00 to 10:10 | | 21 | 9:08 | 8:03 to 11:01 |
| | 22 | 9:08 | 8:03 to 11:01 | | 22 | 9:11 | 8:06 to 11:04 |
| | 23 | 9:11 | 8:06 to 11:04 | | 23 | 10:03 | 8:10 to 11:08 |
| | 24 | 10:02 | 8:09 to 11:07 | | 24 | 10:06 | 9:01 to 11:11 |
| | 25 | 10:06 | 9:01 to 11:11 | | 25 | 10:10 | 9:05 to 12:03 |
| | 26 | 10:09 | 9:04 to 12:02 | | 26 | 11:02 | 9:09 to 12:07 |
| | 27 | 11:01 | 9:08 to 12:06 | | 27 | 11:05 | 10:00 to 12:10 |
| | 28 | 11:04 | 9:11 to 12:09 | | 28 | 11:09 | 10:04 to 13:02 |
| | 29 | 11:07 | 10:02 to 13:00 | e | 29 | 12:01 | 10:08 to 13:06 |
| | 30 | 11:11 | 10:06 to 14:04 | e | 30 | 12:05 | 11:00 to 13:10 |
| e | 31 | 12:03 | 10:10 to 13:08 | e | 31 | 12:08 | 11:03 to 14:01 |
| e | 32 | 12:06 | 11:01 to 13:11 | e | 32 | 13:00 | 11:07 to 14:05 |
| e | 33 | 12:10 | 11:05 to 14:03 | | 33 to 44 | 13:00 + | 11:08 + |
| | 34 to 44 | 13:00 + | 11:06 + | | *** | *** | *** |
| | *** | *** | *** | | *** | *** | *** |
| | *** | *** | *** | | *** | *** | *** |
| | *** | *** | *** | | *** | *** | *** |
| | *** | *** | *** | | *** | *** | *** |
| | *** | *** | *** | | *** | *** | *** |

# Conversion Tables

## National Percentile Ranks and Stanines

**Note:** *The conversion tables for Form 2 have been shaded to help users identify the tables which relate to the standardized form they have been using.*

# Percentile Ranks and Stanines: ACCURACY FORM 1

| Age 6:00 – 6:11 | | | Age 7:00 – 7:11 | | | Age 8:00 – 8:11 | | |
|---|---|---|---|---|---|---|---|---|
| Raw Score | Percentile Rank | Stanine | Raw Score | Percentile Rank | Stanine | Raw Score | Percentile Rank | Stanine |
| 1 | 1 | 1 | 1 | 1 | 1 | *** | *** | *** |
| 2 | 3 | 1 | 2 | 1 | 1 | *** | *** | *** |
| 3 | 5 | 2 | 3 | 2 | 1 | *** | *** | *** |
| 4 | 7 | 2 | 4 | 3 | 1 | *** | *** | *** |
| 5 | 9 | 2 | 5 | 3 | 1 | *** | *** | *** |
| 6 | 12 | 3 | 6 | 4 | 1 | *** | *** | *** |
| 7 | 14 | 3 | 7 | 5 | 2 | *** | *** | *** |
| 8 | 17 | 3 | 8 | 5 | 2 | *** | *** | *** |
| 9 | 20 | 3 | 9 | 7 | 2 | *** | *** | *** |
| 10 | 22 | 3 | 10 | 8 | 2 | 1 to 10 | 1 | 1 |
| 11 | 24 | 4 | 11 | 8 | 2 | 11 | 3 | 1 |
| 12 | 27 | 4 | 12 | 10 | 2 | 12 | 4 | 1 |
| 13 | 30 | 4 | 13 | 12 | 3 | 13 | 5 | 2 |
| 14 | 32 | 4 | 14 | 13 | 3 | 14 | 5 | 2 |
| 15 | 35 | 4 | 15 | 14 | 3 | 15 | 6 | 2 |
| 16 | 37 | 4 | 16 | 16 | 3 | 16 | 6 | 2 |
| 17 | 39 | 4 | 17 | 18 | 3 | 17 | 6 | 2 |
| 18 | 42 | 5 | 18 | 19 | 3 | 18 | 7 | 2 |
| 19 | 43 | 5 | 19 | 21 | 3 | 19 | 8 | 2 |
| 20 | 44 | 5 | 20 | 22 | 3 | 20 | 9 | 2 |
| 21 | 45 | 5 | 21 | 23 | 3 | 21 | 10 | 2 |
| 22 | 48 | 5 | 22 | 25 | 4 | 22 | 11 | 2 |
| 23 | 50 | 5 | 23 | 27 | 4 | 23 | 11 | 2 |
| 24 | 54 | 5 | 24 | 30 | 4 | 24 | 11 | 2 |
| 25 | 58 | 5 | 25 | 32 | 4 | 25 | 13 | 3 |
| 26 | 60 | 5 | 26 | 35 | 4 | 26 | 15 | 3 |
| 27 | 61 | 6 | 27 | 36 | 4 | 27 | 17 | 3 |
| 28 | 62 | 6 | 28 | 37 | 4 | 28 | 18 | 3 |
| 29 | 63 | 6 | 29 | 39 | 4 | 29 | 19 | 3 |
| 30 | 64 | 6 | 30 | 40 | 4 | 30 | 19 | 3 |
| 31 | 66 | 6 | 31 | 41 | 5 | 31 | 19 | 3 |
| 32 | 68 | 6 | 32 | 43 | 5 | 32 | 19 | 3 |
| 33 | 71 | 6 | 33 | 45 | 5 | 33 | 19 | 3 |
| 34 | 71 | 6 | 34 | 47 | 5 | 34 | 20 | 3 |
| 35 | 73 | 6 | 35 | 50 | 5 | 35 | 21 | 3 |
| 36 | 75 | 6 | 36 | 52 | 5 | 36 | 22 | 3 |
| 37 | 77 | 6 | 37 | 56 | 5 | 37 | 24 | 4 |
| 38 | 79 | 7 | 38 | 61 | 6 | 38 | 26 | 4 |
| 39 | 84 | 7 | 39 | 64 | 6 | 39 | 27 | 4 |
| 40 | 86 | 7 | 40 | 66 | 6 | 40 | 29 | 4 |
| 41 | 87 | 7 | 41 | 68 | 6 | 41 | 33 | 4 |
| 42 | 88 | 7 | 42 | 69 | 6 | 42 | 38 | 4 |
| 43 | 91 | 8 | 43 | 70 | 6 | 43 | 41 | 5 |
| 44 | 92 | 8 | 44 | 71 | 6 | 44 | 44 | 5 |
| 45 | 93 | 8 | 45 | 74 | 6 | 45 | 46 | 5 |
| 46 | 93 | 8 | 46 | 77 | 6 | 46 | 49 | 5 |
| 47 | 94 | 8 | 47 | 79 | 7 | 47 | 51 | 5 |
| 48 | 94 | 8 | 48 | 81 | 7 | 48 | 55 | 5 |
| 49 | 94 | 8 | 49 | 82 | 7 | 49 | 58 | 5 |
| 50 | 95 | 8 | 50 | 84 | 7 | 50 | 59 | 5 |

continued on next page

# Percentile Ranks and Stanines: ACCURACY

FORM 1

| Age 6:00 – 6:11 | | | Age 7:00 – 7:11 | | | Age 8:00 – 8:11 | | |
|---|---|---|---|---|---|---|---|---|
| Raw Score | Percentile Rank | Stanine | Raw Score | Percentile Rank | Stanine | Raw Score | Percentile Rank | Stanine |
| 51 | 96 | 8 | 51 | 86 | 7 | 51 | 60 | 5 |
| 52 | 98 | 9 | 52 | 87 | 7 | 52 | 61 | 6 |
| 53 to 100 | 99 | 9 | 53 | 88 | 7 | 53 | 63 | 6 |
| *** | *** | *** | 54 | 88 | 7 | 54 | 64 | 6 |
| *** | *** | *** | 55 | 88 | 7 | 55 | 65 | 6 |
| *** | *** | *** | 56 | 88 | 7 | 56 | 65 | 6 |
| *** | *** | *** | 57 | 89 | 7 | 57 | 66 | 6 |
| *** | *** | *** | 58 | 89 | 7 | 58 | 68 | 6 |
| *** | *** | *** | 59 | 90 | 8 | 59 | 69 | 6 |
| *** | *** | *** | 60 | 90 | 8 | 60 | 70 | 6 |
| *** | *** | *** | 61 | 90 | 8 | 61 | 71 | 6 |
| *** | *** | *** | 62 | 90 | 8 | 62 | 72 | 6 |
| *** | *** | *** | 63 | 91 | 8 | 63 | 73 | 6 |
| *** | *** | *** | 64 | 92 | 8 | 64 | 74 | 6 |
| *** | *** | *** | 65 | 93 | 8 | 65 | 75 | 6 |
| *** | *** | *** | 66 | 93 | 8 | 66 | 76 | 6 |
| *** | *** | *** | 67 | 93 | 8 | 67 | 77 | 6 |
| *** | *** | *** | 68 | 94 | 8 | 68 | 77 | 6 |
| *** | *** | *** | 69 | 95 | 8 | 69 | 77 | 6 |
| *** | *** | *** | 70 | 95 | 8 | 70 | 78 | 7 |
| *** | *** | *** | 71 | 95 | 8 | 71 | 79 | 7 |
| *** | *** | *** | 72 | 95 | 8 | 72 | 80 | 7 |
| *** | *** | *** | 73 | 95 | 8 | 73 | 80 | 7 |
| *** | *** | *** | 74 | 95 | 8 | 74 | 81 | 7 |
| *** | *** | *** | 75 | 96 | 8 | 75 | 82 | 7 |
| *** | *** | *** | 76 | 96 | 8 | 76 | 83 | 7 |
| *** | *** | *** | 77 | 97 | 9 | 77 | 84 | 7 |
| *** | *** | *** | 78 | 97 | 9 | 78 | 85 | 7 |
| *** | *** | *** | 79 | 98 | 9 | 79 | 86 | 7 |
| *** | *** | *** | 80 | 98 | 9 | 80 | 87 | 7 |
| *** | *** | *** | 81 | 98 | 9 | 81 | 88 | 7 |
| *** | *** | *** | 82 | 98 | 9 | 82 | 89 | 7 |
| *** | *** | *** | 83 to 100 | 99 | 9 | 83 | 91 | 8 |
| *** | *** | *** | *** | *** | *** | 84 | 92 | 8 |
| *** | *** | *** | *** | *** | *** | 85 | 93 | 8 |
| *** | *** | *** | *** | *** | *** | 86 | 94 | 8 |
| *** | *** | *** | *** | *** | *** | 87 | 95 | 8 |
| *** | *** | *** | *** | *** | *** | 88 | 96 | 8 |
| *** | *** | *** | *** | *** | *** | 89 | 97 | 9 |
| *** | *** | *** | *** | *** | *** | 90 | 98 | 9 |
| *** | *** | *** | *** | *** | *** | 91 | 98 | 9 |
| *** | *** | *** | *** | *** | *** | 92 | 98 | 9 |
| *** | *** | *** | *** | *** | *** | 93 to 100 | 99 | 9 |
| *** | *** | *** | *** | *** | *** | *** | *** | *** |
| *** | *** | *** | *** | *** | *** | *** | *** | *** |
| *** | *** | *** | *** | *** | *** | *** | *** | *** |
| *** | *** | *** | *** | *** | *** | *** | *** | *** |
| *** | *** | *** | *** | *** | *** | *** | *** | *** |
| *** | *** | *** | *** | *** | *** | *** | *** | *** |

# Percentile Ranks and Stanines: ACCURACY          FORM 1

| Age 9:00 – 9:11 | | | Age 10:00 – 10:11 | | | Age 11:00 – 11:11 | | |
|---|---|---|---|---|---|---|---|---|
| Raw Score | Percentile Rank | Stanine | Raw Score | Percentile Rank | Stanine | Raw Score | Percentile Rank | Stanine |
| *** | *** | *** | *** | *** | *** | *** | *** | *** |
| *** | *** | *** | *** | *** | *** | *** | *** | *** |
| 1 to 13 | 1 | 1 | *** | *** | *** | *** | *** | *** |
| 14 | 2 | 1 | *** | *** | *** | *** | *** | *** |
| 15 | 2 | 1 | *** | *** | *** | *** | *** | *** |
| 16 | 2 | 1 | *** | *** | *** | *** | *** | *** |
| 17 | 2 | 1 | *** | *** | *** | *** | *** | *** |
| 18 | 2 | 1 | *** | *** | *** | *** | *** | *** |
| 19 | 3 | 1 | *** | *** | *** | *** | *** | *** |
| 20 | 3 | 1 | *** | *** | *** | *** | *** | *** |
| 21 | 3 | 1 | *** | *** | *** | *** | *** | *** |
| 22 | 3 | 1 | *** | *** | *** | *** | *** | *** |
| 23 | 3 | 1 | *** | *** | *** | *** | *** | *** |
| 24 | 3 | 1 | *** | *** | *** | *** | *** | *** |
| 25 | 4 | 1 | *** | *** | *** | *** | *** | *** |
| 26 | 4 | 1 | *** | *** | *** | *** | *** | *** |
| 27 | 5 | 2 | *** | *** | *** | *** | *** | *** |
| 28 | 6 | 2 | *** | *** | *** | *** | *** | *** |
| 29 | 7 | 2 | *** | *** | *** | 1 to 29 | 1 | 1 |
| 30 | 8 | 2 | 1 to 30 | 1 | 1 | 30 | 2 | 1 |
| 31 | 9 | 2 | 31 | 2 | 1 | 31 | 2 | 1 |
| 32 | 11 | 2 | 32 | 2 | 1 | 32 | 2 | 1 |
| 33 | 12 | 3 | 33 | 2 | 1 | 33 | 2 | 1 |
| 34 | 12 | 3 | 34 | 2 | 1 | 34 | 2 | 1 |
| 35 | 13 | 3 | 35 | 3 | 1 | 35 | 3 | 1 |
| 36 | 14 | 3 | 36 | 5 | 2 | 36 | 3 | 1 |
| 37 | 16 | 3 | 37 | 6 | 2 | 37 | 4 | 1 |
| 38 | 18 | 3 | 38 | 6 | 2 | 38 | 4 | 1 |
| 39 | 19 | 3 | 39 | 8 | 2 | 39 | 4 | 1 |
| 40 | 21 | 3 | 40 | 9 | 2 | 40 | 4 | 1 |
| 41 | 23 | 3 | 41 | 10 | 2 | 41 | 5 | 2 |
| 42 | 26 | 4 | 42 | 12 | 3 | 42 | 5 | 2 |
| 43 | 28 | 4 | 43 | 13 | 3 | 43 | 5 | 2 |
| 44 | 31 | 4 | 44 | 16 | 3 | 44 | 7 | 2 |
| 45 | 33 | 4 | 45 | 18 | 3 | 45 | 10 | 2 |
| 46 | 36 | 4 | 46 | 18 | 3 | 46 | 12 | 3 |
| 47 | 38 | 4 | 47 | 19 | 3 | 47 | 13 | 3 |
| 48 | 40 | 4 | 48 | 20 | 3 | 48 | 13 | 3 |
| 49 | 41 | 5 | 49 | 20 | 3 | 49 | 14 | 3 |
| 50 | 41 | 5 | 50 | 21 | 3 | 50 | 14 | 3 |
| 51 | 42 | 5 | 51 | 21 | 3 | 51 | 15 | 3 |
| 52 | 44 | 5 | 52 | 22 | 3 | 52 | 16 | 3 |
| 53 | 44 | 5 | 53 | 23 | 3 | 53 | 16 | 3 |
| 54 | 45 | 5 | 54 | 25 | 4 | 54 | 16 | 3 |
| 55 | 45 | 5 | 55 | 26 | 4 | 55 | 17 | 3 |
| 56 | 47 | 5 | 56 | 26 | 4 | 56 | 19 | 3 |
| 57 | 48 | 5 | 57 | 26 | 4 | 57 | 20 | 3 |
| 58 | 49 | 5 | 58 | 27 | 4 | 58 | 21 | 3 |
| 59 | 52 | 5 | 59 | 28 | 4 | 59 | 21 | 3 |
| 60 | 53 | 5 | 60 | 30 | 4 | 60 | 22 | 3 |

continued on next page

# Percentile Ranks and Stanines: ACCURACY

FORM 1

| Age 9:00 – 9:11 | | | Age 10:00 – 10:11 | | | Age 11:00 – 11:11 | | |
|---|---|---|---|---|---|---|---|---|
| Raw Score | Percentile Rank | Stanine | Raw Score | Percentile Rank | Stanine | Raw Score | Percentile Rank | Stanine |
| 61 | 54 | 5 | 61 | 31 | 4 | 61 | 22 | 3 |
| 62 | 55 | 5 | 62 | 32 | 4 | 62 | 23 | 3 |
| 63 | 57 | 5 | 63 | 33 | 4 | 63 | 23 | 3 |
| 64 | 58 | 5 | 64 | 33 | 4 | 64 | 24 | 4 |
| 65 | 59 | 5 | 65 | 35 | 4 | 65 | 26 | 4 |
| 66 | 61 | 6 | 66 | 36 | 4 | 66 | 26 | 4 |
| 67 | 62 | 6 | 67 | 37 | 4 | 67 | 27 | 4 |
| 68 | 62 | 6 | 68 | 39 | 4 | 68 | 29 | 4 |
| 69 | 63 | 6 | 69 | 41 | 5 | 69 | 30 | 4 |
| 70 | 64 | 6 | 70 | 41 | 5 | 70 | 32 | 4 |
| 71 | 65 | 6 | 71 | 42 | 5 | 71 | 32 | 4 |
| 72 | 66 | 6 | 72 | 44 | 5 | 72 | 34 | 4 |
| 73 | 66 | 6 | 73 | 45 | 5 | 73 | 35 | 4 |
| 74 | 67 | 6 | 74 | 46 | 5 | 74 | 36 | 4 |
| 75 | 68 | 6 | 75 | 48 | 5 | 75 | 38 | 4 |
| 76 | 71 | 6 | 76 | 51 | 5 | 76 | 40 | 4 |
| 77 | 74 | 6 | 77 | 53 | 5 | 77 | 43 | 5 |
| 78 | 75 | 6 | 78 | 55 | 5 | 78 | 45 | 5 |
| 79 | 76 | 6 | 79 | 58 | 5 | 79 | 47 | 5 |
| 80 | 79 | 7 | 80 | 59 | 5 | 80 | 50 | 5 |
| 81 | 81 | 7 | 81 | 61 | 6 | 81 | 52 | 5 |
| 82 | 84 | 7 | 82 | 63 | 6 | 82 | 53 | 5 |
| 83 | 85 | 7 | 83 | 64 | 6 | 83 | 54 | 5 |
| 84 | 87 | 7 | 84 | 64 | 6 | 84 | 56 | 5 |
| 85 | 88 | 7 | 85 | 65 | 6 | 85 | 57 | 5 |
| 86 | 89 | 7 | 86 | 66 | 6 | 86 | 60 | 5 |
| 87 | 90 | 8 | 87 | 67 | 6 | 87 | 63 | 6 |
| 88 | 90 | 8 | 88 | 70 | 6 | 88 | 65 | 6 |
| 89 | 91 | 8 | 89 | 74 | 6 | 89 | 67 | 6 |
| 90 | 93 | 8 | 90 | 78 | 7 | 90 | 70 | 6 |
| 91 | 94 | 8 | 91 | 81 | 7 | 91 | 73 | 6 |
| 92 | 95 | 8 | 92 | 83 | 7 | 92 | 76 | 6 |
| 93 | 96 | 8 | 93 | 85 | 7 | 93 | 79 | 7 |
| 94 | 97 | 9 | 94 | 87 | 7 | 94 | 83 | 7 |
| 95 | 97 | 9 | 95 | 90 | 8 | 95 | 85 | 7 |
| 96 | 98 | 9 | 96 | 92 | 8 | 96 | 87 | 7 |
| 97 | 98 | 9 | 97 | 95 | 8 | 97 | 89 | 7 |
| 98 | 98 | 9 | 98 | 97 | 9 | 98 | 92 | 8 |
| 99 | 99 | 9 | 99 | 98 | 9 | 99 | 95 | 8 |
| 100 | 99 | 9 | 100 | 99 | 9 | 100 | 97 | 9 |

# Percentile Ranks and Stanines: RATE

FORM 1

| Age 6:00 – 6:11 | | | Age 7:00 – 7:11 | | | Age 8:00 – 8:11 | | |
|---|---|---|---|---|---|---|---|---|
| Raw Score | Percentile Rank | Stanine | Raw Score | Percentile Rank | Stanine | Raw Score | Percentile Rank | Stanine |
| *** | *** | *** | *** | *** | *** | *** | *** | *** |
| *** | *** | *** | *** | *** | *** | *** | *** | *** |
| *** | *** | *** | *** | *** | *** | *** | *** | *** |
| *** | *** | *** | *** | *** | *** | *** | *** | *** |
| *** | *** | *** | *** | *** | *** | *** | *** | *** |
| *** | *** | *** | *** | *** | *** | *** | *** | *** |
| 1 to 7 | 1 | 1 | *** | *** | *** | *** | *** | *** |
| 8 | 2 | 1 | 1 to 8 | 1 | 1 | *** | *** | *** |
| 9 | 4 | 1 | 9 | 2 | 1 | *** | *** | *** |
| 10 | 7 | 2 | 10 | 3 | 1 | *** | *** | *** |
| 11 | 8 | 2 | 11 | 3 | 1 | *** | *** | *** |
| 12 | 8 | 2 | 12 | 3 | 1 | *** | *** | *** |
| 13 | 10 | 2 | 13 | 4 | 1 | 1 to 13 | 1 | 1 |
| 14 | 13 | 3 | 14 | 5 | 2 | 14 | 2 | 1 |
| 15 | 14 | 3 | 15 | 6 | 2 | 15 | 3 | 1 |
| 16 | 15 | 3 | 16 | 8 | 2 | 16 | 3 | 1 |
| 17 | 16 | 3 | 17 | 9 | 2 | 17 | 3 | 1 |
| 18 | 17 | 3 | 18 | 9 | 2 | 18 | 4 | 1 |
| 19 | 18 | 3 | 19 | 10 | 2 | 19 | 4 | 1 |
| 20 | 20 | 3 | 20 | 12 | 3 | 20 | 4 | 1 |
| 21 | 22 | 3 | 21 | 12 | 3 | 21 | 4 | 1 |
| 22 | 24 | 4 | 22 | 12 | 3 | 22 | 5 | 2 |
| 23 | 25 | 4 | 23 | 13 | 3 | 23 | 6 | 2 |
| 24 | 27 | 4 | 24 | 14 | 3 | 24 | 7 | 2 |
| 25 | 30 | 4 | 25 | 14 | 3 | 25 | 7 | 2 |
| 26 | 33 | 4 | 26 | 15 | 3 | 26 | 7 | 2 |
| 27 | 36 | 4 | 27 | 15 | 3 | 27 | 7 | 2 |
| 28 | 38 | 4 | 28 | 17 | 3 | 28 | 8 | 2 |
| 29 | 39 | 4 | 29 | 18 | 3 | 29 | 8 | 2 |
| 30 | 42 | 5 | 30 | 21 | 3 | 30 | 9 | 2 |
| 31 | 44 | 5 | 31 | 22 | 3 | 31 | 10 | 2 |
| 32 | 45 | 5 | 32 | 23 | 3 | 32 | 11 | 2 |
| 33 | 46 | 5 | 33 | 25 | 4 | 33 | 12 | 3 |
| 34 | 47 | 5 | 34 | 27 | 4 | 34 | 13 | 3 |
| 35 | 48 | 5 | 35 | 28 | 4 | 35 | 13 | 3 |
| 36 | 50 | 5 | 36 | 30 | 4 | 36 | 14 | 3 |
| 37 | 51 | 5 | 37 | 32 | 4 | 37 | 14 | 3 |
| 38 | 52 | 5 | 38 | 35 | 4 | 38 | 15 | 3 |
| 39 | 54 | 5 | 39 | 37 | 4 | 39 | 16 | 3 |
| 40 | 56 | 5 | 40 | 39 | 4 | 40 | 18 | 3 |
| 41 | 58 | 5 | 41 | 41 | 5 | 41 | 19 | 3 |
| 42 | 59 | 5 | 42 | 43 | 5 | 42 | 20 | 3 |
| 43 | 60 | 5 | 43 | 44 | 5 | 43 | 20 | 3 |
| 44 | 62 | 6 | 44 | 45 | 5 | 44 | 21 | 3 |
| 45 | 63 | 6 | 45 | 47 | 5 | 45 | 23 | 3 |
| 46 | 65 | 6 | 46 | 49 | 5 | 46 | 24 | 4 |
| 47 | 67 | 6 | 47 | 51 | 5 | 47 | 24 | 4 |
| 48 | 69 | 6 | 48 | 53 | 5 | 48 | 25 | 4 |
| 49 | 70 | 6 | 49 | 54 | 5 | 49 | 26 | 4 |
| 50 | 71 | 6 | 50 | 55 | 5 | 50 | 27 | 4 |

continued on next page

# Percentile Ranks and Stanines: RATE

| Age 6:00 – 6:11 | | | Age 7:00 – 7:11 | | | Age 8:00 – 8:11 | | |
|---|---|---|---|---|---|---|---|---|
| Raw Score | Percentile Rank | Stanine | Raw Score | Percentile Rank | Stanine | Raw Score | Percentile Rank | Stanine |
| 51 | 74 | 6 | 51 | 57 | 5 | 51 | 28 | 4 |
| 52 | 76 | 6 | 52 | 58 | 5 | 52 | 30 | 4 |
| 53 | 77 | 6 | 53 | 58 | 5 | 53 | 31 | 4 |
| 54 | 77 | 6 | 54 | 59 | 5 | 54 | 32 | 4 |
| 55 | 77 | 6 | 55 | 60 | 5 | 55 | 34 | 4 |
| 56 | 78 | 7 | 56 | 61 | 6 | 56 | 36 | 4 |
| 57 | 78 | 7 | 57 | 63 | 6 | 57 | 39 | 4 |
| 58 | 78 | 7 | 58 | 64 | 6 | 58 | 41 | 5 |
| 59 | 79 | 7 | 59 | 66 | 6 | 59 | 43 | 5 |
| 60 | 79 | 7 | 60 | 68 | 6 | 60 | 44 | 5 |
| 61 | 80 | 7 | 61 | 68 | 6 | 61 | 45 | 5 |
| 62 | 82 | 7 | 62 | 68 | 6 | 62 | 46 | 5 |
| 63 | 83 | 7 | 63 | 70 | 6 | 63 | 47 | 5 |
| 64 | 83 | 7 | 64 | 72 | 6 | 64 | 48 | 5 |
| 65 | 83 | 7 | 65 | 72 | 6 | 65 | 48 | 5 |
| 66 | 84 | 7 | 66 | 72 | 6 | 66 | 49 | 5 |
| 67 | 85 | 7 | 67 | 73 | 6 | 67 | 50 | 5 |
| 68 | 85 | 7 | 68 | 74 | 6 | 68 | 51 | 5 |
| 69 | 85 | 7 | 69 | 75 | 6 | 69 | 51 | 5 |
| 70 | 86 | 7 | 70 | 75 | 6 | 70 | 53 | 5 |
| 71 | 87 | 7 | 71 | 76 | 6 | 71 | 54 | 5 |
| 72 | 88 | 7 | 72 | 77 | 6 | 72 | 56 | 5 |
| 73 | 89 | 7 | 73 | 78 | 7 | 73 | 58 | 5 |
| 74 | 90 | 8 | 74 | 79 | 7 | 74 | 60 | 5 |
| 75 | 90 | 8 | 75 | 79 | 7 | 75 | 61 | 6 |
| 76 | 90 | 8 | 76 | 80 | 7 | 76 | 63 | 6 |
| 77 | 90 | 8 | 77 | 81 | 7 | 77 | 64 | 6 |
| 78 | 91 | 8 | 78 | 82 | 7 | 78 | 66 | 6 |
| 79 | 92 | 8 | 79 | 82 | 7 | 79 | 68 | 6 |
| 80 | 92 | 8 | 80 | 82 | 7 | 80 | 70 | 6 |
| 81 | 92 | 8 | 81 | 83 | 7 | 81 | 71 | 6 |
| 82 | 93 | 8 | 82 | 84 | 7 | 82 | 74 | 6 |
| 83 | 94 | 8 | 83 | 85 | 7 | 83 | 76 | 6 |
| 84 | 94 | 8 | 84 | 86 | 7 | 84 | 77 | 6 |
| 85 | 94 | 8 | 85 | 87 | 7 | 85 | 78 | 7 |
| 86 | 94 | 8 | 86 | 87 | 7 | 86 | 79 | 7 |
| 87 | 94 | 8 | 87 | 87 | 7 | 87 | 80 | 7 |
| 88 | 95 | 8 | 88 | 88 | 7 | 88 | 80 | 7 |
| 89 | 95 | 8 | 89 | 89 | 7 | 89 | 81 | 7 |
| 90 | 95 | 8 | 90 | 89 | 7 | 90 | 83 | 7 |
| 91 | 95 | 8 | 91 | 89 | 7 | 91 | 84 | 7 |
| 92 | 95 | 8 | 92 | 90 | 8 | 92 | 84 | 7 |
| 93 | 95 | 8 | 93 | 90 | 8 | 93 | 86 | 7 |
| 94 | 95 | 8 | 94 | 91 | 8 | 94 | 87 | 7 |
| 95 | 95 | 8 | 95 | 92 | 8 | 95 | 88 | 7 |
| 96 | 95 | 8 | 96 | 92 | 8 | 96 | 89 | 7 |
| 97 | 95 | 8 | 97 | 92 | 8 | 97 | 90 | 8 |
| 98 | 95 | 8 | 98 | 93 | 8 | 98 | 91 | 8 |
| 99 | 95 | 8 | 99 | 93 | 8 | 99 | 91 | 8 |
| 100 | 95 | 8 | 100 | 93 | 8 | 100 | 91 | 8 |

continued on next page

## Percentile Ranks and Stanines: RATE

| Age 6:00 – 6:11 | | | Age 7:00 – 7:11 | | | Age 8:00 – 8:11 | | |
|---|---|---|---|---|---|---|---|---|
| Raw Score | Percentile Rank | Stanine | Raw Score | Percentile Rank | Stanine | Raw Score | Percentile Rank | Stanine |
| 101 | 95 | 8 | 101 | 93 | 8 | 101 | 91 | 8 |
| 102 | 95 | 8 | 102 | 93 | 8 | 102 | 92 | 8 |
| 103 | 95 | 8 | 103 | 93 | 8 | 103 | 94 | 8 |
| 104 | 96 | 8 | 104 | 94 | 8 | 104 | 94 | 8 |
| 105 | 96 | 8 | 105 | 94 | 8 | 105 | 94 | 8 |
| 106 | 97 | 9 | 106 | 94 | 8 | 106 | 94 | 8 |
| 107 | 97 | 9 | 107 | 94 | 8 | 107 | 94 | 8 |
| 108 | 97 | 9 | 108 | 95 | 8 | 108 | 94 | 8 |
| 109 | 98 | 9 | 109 | 96 | 8 | 109 | 95 | 8 |
| 110+ | 99 | 9 | 110 | 96 | 8 | 110 | 95 | 8 |
| *** | *** | *** | 111 | 96 | 8 | 111 | 95 | 8 |
| *** | *** | *** | 112 | 97 | 9 | 112 | 95 | 8 |
| *** | *** | *** | 113 | 97 | 9 | 113 | 95 | 8 |
| *** | *** | *** | 114 | 97 | 9 | 114 | 95 | 8 |
| *** | *** | *** | 115 | 97 | 9 | 115 | 95 | 8 |
| *** | *** | *** | 116 | 97 | 9 | 116 | 96 | 8 |
| *** | *** | *** | 117 | 97 | 9 | 117 | 96 | 8 |
| *** | *** | *** | 118 | 98 | 9 | 118 | 96 | 8 |
| *** | *** | *** | 119 | 98 | 9 | 119 | 97 | 9 |
| *** | *** | *** | 120 | 98 | 9 | 120 | 97 | 9 |
| *** | *** | *** | 121 | 98 | 9 | 121 | 97 | 9 |
| *** | *** | *** | 122 | 98 | 9 | 122 | 97 | 9 |
| *** | *** | *** | 123 | 98 | 9 | 123 | 97 | 9 |
| *** | *** | *** | 124 | 98 | 9 | 124 | 97 | 9 |
| *** | *** | *** | 125 | 98 | 9 | 125 | 97 | 9 |
| *** | *** | *** | 126 | 98 | 9 | 126 | 98 | 9 |
| *** | *** | *** | 127+ | 99 | 9 | 127 | 98 | 9 |
| *** | *** | *** | *** | *** | *** | 128 | 98 | 9 |
| *** | *** | *** | *** | *** | *** | 129 | 98 | 9 |
| *** | *** | *** | *** | *** | *** | 130+ | 99 | 9 |

# Percentile Ranks and Stanines: RATE

FORM 1

| Age 9:00 – 9:11 | | | Age 10:00 – 10:11 | | | Age 11:00 – 11:11 | | |
|---|---|---|---|---|---|---|---|---|
| Raw Score | Percentile Rank | Stanine | Raw Score | Percentile Rank | Stanine | Raw Score | Percentile Rank | Stanine |
| * * * | * * * | * * * | * * * | * * * | * * * | * * * | * * * | * * * |
| * * * | * * * | * * * | * * * | * * * | * * * | * * * | * * * | * * * |
| * * * | * * * | * * * | * * * | * * * | * * * | * * * | * * * | * * * |
| * * * | * * * | * * * | * * * | * * * | * * * | * * * | * * * | * * * |
| 1 to 25 | 1 | 1 | * * * | * * * | * * * | * * * | * * * | * * * |
| 26 | 2 | 1 | * * * | * * * | * * * | * * * | * * * | * * * |
| 27 | 3 | 1 | * * * | * * * | * * * | * * * | * * * | * * * |
| 28 | 3 | 1 | * * * | * * * | * * * | * * * | * * * | * * * |
| 29 | 3 | 1 | * * * | * * * | * * * | * * * | * * * | * * * |
| 30 | 3 | 1 | * * * | * * * | * * * | 1 to 30 | 1 | 1 |
| 31 | 3 | 1 | 1 to 31 | 1 | 1 | 31 | 2 | 1 |
| 32 | 4 | 1 | 32 | 2 | 1 | 32 | 2 | 1 |
| 33 | 4 | 1 | 33 | 3 | 1 | 33 | 2 | 1 |
| 34 | 4 | 1 | 34 | 3 | 1 | 34 | 2 | 1 |
| 35 | 4 | 1 | 35 | 3 | 1 | 35 | 2 | 1 |
| 36 | 5 | 2 | 36 | 3 | 1 | 36 | 3 | 1 |
| 37 | 5 | 2 | 37 | 3 | 1 | 37 | 3 | 1 |
| 38 | 6 | 2 | 38 | 3 | 1 | 38 | 3 | 1 |
| 39 | 7 | 2 | 39 | 4 | 1 | 39 | 4 | 1 |
| 40 | 7 | 2 | 40 | 5 | 2 | 40 | 4 | 1 |
| 41 | 7 | 2 | 41 | 6 | 2 | 41 | 4 | 1 |
| 42 | 7 | 2 | 42 | 7 | 2 | 42 | 5 | 2 |
| 43 | 8 | 2 | 43 | 7 | 2 | 43 | 6 | 2 |
| 44 | 10 | 2 | 44 | 8 | 2 | 44 | 6 | 2 |
| 45 | 10 | 2 | 45 | 8 | 2 | 45 | 7 | 2 |
| 46 | 10 | 2 | 46 | 9 | 2 | 46 | 7 | 2 |
| 47 | 12 | 3 | 47 | 9 | 2 | 47 | 8 | 2 |
| 48 | 13 | 3 | 48 | 10 | 2 | 48 | 8 | 2 |
| 49 | 14 | 3 | 49 | 11 | 2 | 49 | 8 | 2 |
| 50 | 15 | 3 | 50 | 12 | 3 | 50 | 9 | 2 |
| 51 | 17 | 3 | 51 | 13 | 3 | 51 | 9 | 2 |
| 52 | 19 | 3 | 52 | 14 | 3 | 52 | 9 | 2 |
| 53 | 20 | 3 | 53 | 15 | 3 | 53 | 10 | 2 |
| 54 | 22 | 3 | 54 | 16 | 3 | 54 | 11 | 2 |
| 55 | 24 | 4 | 55 | 17 | 3 | 55 | 11 | 2 |
| 56 | 25 | 4 | 56 | 18 | 3 | 56 | 11 | 2 |
| 57 | 26 | 4 | 57 | 20 | 3 | 57 | 12 | 3 |
| 58 | 28 | 4 | 58 | 23 | 3 | 58 | 13 | 3 |
| 59 | 28 | 4 | 59 | 25 | 4 | 59 | 14 | 3 |
| 60 | 30 | 4 | 60 | 26 | 4 | 60 | 16 | 3 |
| 61 | 32 | 4 | 61 | 26 | 4 | 61 | 19 | 3 |
| 62 | 33 | 4 | 62 | 27 | 4 | 62 | 20 | 3 |
| 63 | 35 | 4 | 63 | 28 | 4 | 63 | 21 | 3 |
| 64 | 38 | 4 | 64 | 28 | 4 | 64 | 22 | 3 |
| 65 | 39 | 4 | 65 | 29 | 4 | 65 | 22 | 3 |
| 66 | 42 | 5 | 66 | 29 | 4 | 66 | 23 | 3 |
| 67 | 44 | 5 | 67 | 32 | 4 | 67 | 24 | 4 |
| 68 | 45 | 5 | 68 | 33 | 4 | 68 | 25 | 4 |
| 69 | 47 | 5 | 69 | 34 | 4 | 69 | 25 | 4 |
| 70 | 49 | 5 | 70 | 34 | 4 | 70 | 25 | 4 |

continued on next page

## Percentile Ranks and Stanines: RATE

FORM 1

| Age 9:00 – 9:11 | | | Age 10:00 – 10:11 | | | Age 11:00 – 11:11 | | |
|---|---|---|---|---|---|---|---|---|
| Raw Score | Percentile Rank | Stanine | Raw Score | Percentile Rank | Stanine | Raw Score | Percentile Rank | Stanine |
| 71 | 51 | 5 | 71 | 35 | 4 | 71 | 26 | 4 |
| 72 | 52 | 5 | 72 | 36 | 4 | 72 | 28 | 4 |
| 73 | 53 | 5 | 73 | 36 | 4 | 73 | 28 | 4 |
| 74 | 55 | 5 | 74 | 37 | 4 | 74 | 29 | 4 |
| 75 | 59 | 5 | 75 | 39 | 4 | 75 | 29 | 4 |
| 76 | 61 | 6 | 76 | 40 | 4 | 76 | 30 | 4 |
| 77 | 62 | 6 | 77 | 41 | 5 | 77 | 30 | 4 |
| 78 | 63 | 6 | 78 | 42 | 5 | 78 | 32 | 4 |
| 79 | 64 | 6 | 79 | 44 | 5 | 79 | 33 | 4 |
| 80 | 65 | 6 | 80 | 47 | 5 | 80 | 33 | 4 |
| 81 | 66 | 6 | 81 | 49 | 5 | 81 | 34 | 4 |
| 82 | 68 | 6 | 82 | 51 | 5 | 82 | 36 | 4 |
| 83 | 69 | 6 | 83 | 51 | 5 | 83 | 38 | 4 |
| 84 | 71 | 6 | 84 | 52 | 5 | 84 | 39 | 4 |
| 85 | 71 | 6 | 85 | 53 | 5 | 85 | 40 | 4 |
| 86 | 71 | 6 | 86 | 55 | 5 | 86 | 42 | 5 |
| 87 | 72 | 6 | 87 | 57 | 5 | 87 | 44 | 5 |
| 88 | 74 | 6 | 88 | 58 | 5 | 88 | 46 | 5 |
| 89 | 75 | 6 | 89 | 59 | 5 | 89 | 48 | 5 |
| 90 | 77 | 6 | 90 | 59 | 5 | 90 | 49 | 5 |
| 91 | 79 | 7 | 91 | 60 | 5 | 91 | 50 | 5 |
| 92 | 80 | 7 | 92 | 60 | 5 | 92 | 50 | 5 |
| 93 | 81 | 7 | 93 | 60 | 5 | 93 | 51 | 5 |
| 94 | 82 | 7 | 94 | 61 | 6 | 94 | 53 | 5 |
| 95 | 83 | 7 | 95 | 62 | 6 | 95 | 54 | 5 |
| 96 | 84 | 7 | 96 | 63 | 6 | 96 | 57 | 5 |
| 97 | 85 | 7 | 97 | 64 | 6 | 97 | 60 | 5 |
| 98 | 86 | 7 | 98 | 64 | 6 | 98 | 63 | 6 |
| 99 | 86 | 7 | 99 | 66 | 6 | 99 | 64 | 6 |
| 100 | 86 | 7 | 100 | 67 | 6 | 100 | 65 | 6 |
| 101 | 86 | 7 | 101 | 69 | 6 | 101 | 66 | 6 |
| 102 | 87 | 7 | 102 | 70 | 6 | 102 | 68 | 6 |
| 103 | 88 | 7 | 103 | 71 | 6 | 103 | 69 | 6 |
| 104 | 88 | 7 | 104 | 72 | 6 | 104 | 69 | 6 |
| 105 | 89 | 7 | 105 | 74 | 6 | 105 | 70 | 6 |
| 106 | 90 | 8 | 106 | 76 | 6 | 106 | 71 | 6 |
| 107 | 91 | 8 | 107 | 78 | 7 | 107 | 71 | 6 |
| 108 | 91 | 8 | 108 | 79 | 7 | 108 | 73 | 6 |
| 109 | 91 | 8 | 109 | 80 | 7 | 109 | 75 | 6 |
| 110 | 92 | 8 | 110 | 81 | 7 | 110 | 76 | 6 |
| 111 | 93 | 8 | 111 | 82 | 7 | 111 | 77 | 6 |
| 112 | 94 | 8 | 112 | 83 | 7 | 112 | 78 | 7 |
| 113 | 94 | 8 | 113 | 83 | 7 | 113 | 78 | 7 |
| 114 | 94 | 8 | 114 | 84 | 7 | 114 | 79 | 7 |
| 115 | 95 | 8 | 115 | 84 | 7 | 115 | 79 | 7 |
| 116 | 95 | 8 | 116 | 86 | 7 | 116 | 80 | 7 |
| 117 | 96 | 8 | 117 | 86 | 7 | 117 | 80 | 7 |
| 118 | 96 | 8 | 118 | 87 | 7 | 118 | 81 | 7 |
| 119 | 96 | 8 | 119 | 88 | 7 | 119 | 82 | 7 |
| 120 | 96 | 8 | 120 | 90 | 8 | 120 | 82 | 7 |

continued on next page

# Percentile Ranks and Stanines: RATE

FORM 1

| Age 9:00 – 9:11 | | | Age 10:00 – 10:11 | | | Age 11:00 – 11:11 | | |
|---|---|---|---|---|---|---|---|---|
| Raw Score | Percentile Rank | Stanine | Raw Score | Percentile Rank | Stanine | Raw Score | Percentile Rank | Stanine |
| 121 | 96 | 8 | 121 | 91 | 8 | 121 | 82 | 7 |
| 122 | 96 | 8 | 122 | 91 | 8 | 122 | 83 | 7 |
| 123 | 96 | 8 | 123 | 92 | 8 | 123 | 83 | 7 |
| 124 | 97 | 9 | 124 | 92 | 8 | 124 | 84 | 7 |
| 125 | 97 | 9 | 125 | 92 | 8 | 125 | 84 | 7 |
| 126 | 97 | 9 | 126 | 93 | 8 | 126 | 84 | 7 |
| 127 | 98 | 9 | 127 | 94 | 8 | 127 | 85 | 7 |
| 128 | 98 | 9 | 128 | 95 | 8 | 128 | 87 | 7 |
| 129 | 98 | 9 | 129 | 96 | 8 | 129 | 89 | 7 |
| 130 + | 99 | 9 | 130 | 96 | 8 | 130 | 90 | 8 |
| *** | *** | *** | 131 | 96 | 8 | 131 | 91 | 8 |
| *** | *** | *** | 132 | 96 | 8 | 132 | 93 | 8 |
| *** | *** | *** | 133 | 97 | 9 | 133 | 93 | 8 |
| *** | *** | *** | 134 | 98 | 9 | 134 | 94 | 8 |
| *** | *** | *** | 135 | 98 | 9 | 135 | 94 | 8 |
| *** | *** | *** | 136 | 98 | 9 | 136 | 94 | 8 |
| *** | *** | *** | 137 | 98 | 9 | 137 | 94 | 8 |
| *** | *** | *** | 138 | 98 | 9 | 138 | 95 | 8 |
| *** | *** | *** | 139 | 98 | 9 | 139 | 96 | 8 |
| *** | *** | *** | 140 | 98 | 9 | 140 | 96 | 8 |
| *** | *** | *** | 141 | 98 | 9 | 141 | 96 | 8 |
| *** | *** | *** | 142 | 98 | 9 | 142 | 96 | 8 |
| *** | *** | *** | 143 | 98 | 9 | 143 | 96 | 8 |
| *** | *** | *** | 144 | 98 | 9 | 144 | 96 | 8 |
| *** | *** | *** | 145 | 98 | 9 | 145 | 96 | 8 |
| *** | *** | *** | 146 | 98 | 9 | 146 | 97 | 9 |
| *** | *** | *** | 147 | 98 | 9 | 147 | 97 | 9 |
| *** | *** | *** | 148 | 98 | 9 | 148 | 97 | 9 |
| *** | *** | *** | 149 | 98 | 9 | 149 | 97 | 9 |
| *** | *** | *** | 150 + | 99 | 9 | 150 | 97 | 9 |
| *** | *** | *** | *** | *** | *** | 151 | 98 | 9 |
| *** | *** | *** | *** | *** | *** | 152 | 98 | 9 |
| *** | *** | *** | *** | *** | *** | 153 + | 99 | 9 |
| *** | *** | *** | *** | *** | *** | *** | *** | *** |
| *** | *** | *** | *** | *** | *** | *** | *** | *** |
| *** | *** | *** | *** | *** | *** | *** | *** | *** |
| *** | *** | *** | *** | *** | *** | *** | *** | *** |
| *** | *** | *** | *** | *** | *** | *** | *** | *** |
| *** | *** | *** | *** | *** | *** | *** | *** | *** |
| *** | *** | *** | *** | *** | *** | *** | *** | *** |

## Percentile Ranks and Stanines: COMPREHENSION FORM 1

| Age 6:00 – 6:11 | | | Age 7:00 – 7:11 | | | Age 8:00 – 8:11 | | |
|---|---|---|---|---|---|---|---|---|
| Raw Score | Percentile Rank | Stanine | Raw Score | Percentile Rank | Stanine | Raw Score | Percentile Rank | Stanine |
| 1 | 2 | 1 | 1 | 1 | 1 | *** | *** | *** |
| 2 | 10 | 2 | 2 | 4 | 1 | *** | *** | *** |
| 3 | 20 | 3 | 3 | 8 | 2 | 1 to 3 | 1 | 1 |
| 4 | 27 | 4 | 4 | 10 | 2 | 4 | 3 | 1 |
| 5 | 30 | 4 | 5 | 12 | 3 | 5 | 5 | 2 |
| 6 | 31 | 4 | 6 | 14 | 3 | 6 | 5 | 2 |
| 7 | 39 | 4 | 7 | 19 | 3 | 7 | 8 | 2 |
| 8 | 48 | 5 | 8 | 26 | 4 | 8 | 11 | 2 |
| 9 | 54 | 5 | 9 | 31 | 4 | 9 | 15 | 3 |
| 10 | 59 | 5 | 10 | 37 | 4 | 10 | 18 | 3 |
| 11 | 65 | 6 | 11 | 46 | 5 | 11 | 22 | 3 |
| 12 | 72 | 6 | 12 | 53 | 5 | 12 | 26 | 4 |
| 13 | 77 | 6 | 13 | 59 | 5 | 13 | 29 | 4 |
| 14 | 80 | 7 | 14 | 63 | 6 | 14 | 34 | 4 |
| 15 | 82 | 7 | 15 | 71 | 6 | 15 | 40 | 4 |
| 16 | 84 | 7 | 16 | 78 | 7 | 16 | 45 | 5 |
| 17 | 86 | 7 | 17 | 81 | 7 | 17 | 51 | 5 |
| 18 | 90 | 8 | 18 | 83 | 7 | 18 | 56 | 5 |
| 19 | 93 | 8 | 19 | 86 | 7 | 19 | 63 | 6 |
| 20 | 95 | 8 | 20 | 89 | 7 | 20 | 68 | 6 |
| 21 | 95 | 8 | 21 | 90 | 8 | 21 | 71 | 6 |
| 22 | 96 | 8 | 22 | 92 | 8 | 22 | 73 | 6 |
| 23 | 96 | 8 | 23 | 94 | 8 | 23 | 75 | 6 |
| 24 | 97 | 9 | 24 | 95 | 8 | 24 | 77 | 6 |
| 25 | 97 | 9 | 25 | 95 | 8 | 25 | 80 | 7 |
| 26 | 97 | 9 | 26 | 95 | 8 | 26 | 83 | 7 |
| 27 | 97 | 9 | 27 | 95 | 8 | 27 | 85 | 7 |
| 28 | 97 | 9 | 28 | 96 | 8 | 28 | 87 | 7 |
| 29 | 97 | 9 | 29 | 96 | 8 | 29 | 89 | 7 |
| 30 | 98 | 9 | 30 | 97 | 9 | 30 | 90 | 8 |
| 31 to 44 | 99 | 9 | 31 | 98 | 9 | 31 | 91 | 8 |
| *** | *** | *** | 32 | 98 | 9 | 32 | 93 | 8 |
| *** | *** | *** | 33 | 98 | 9 | 33 | 95 | 8 |
| *** | *** | *** | 34 | 98 | 9 | 34 | 96 | 8 |
| *** | *** | *** | 35 | 98 | 9 | 35 | 98 | 9 |
| *** | *** | *** | 36 to 44 | 99 | 9 | 36 to 44 | 99 | 9 |
| *** | *** | *** | *** | *** | *** | *** | *** | *** |
| *** | *** | *** | *** | *** | *** | *** | *** | *** |
| *** | *** | *** | *** | *** | *** | *** | *** | *** |
| *** | *** | *** | *** | *** | *** | *** | *** | *** |

# Percentile Ranks and Stanines: COMPREHENSION     FORM 1

| Age 9:00 – 9:11 | | | Age 10:00 – 10:11 | | | Age 11:00 – 11:11 | | |
|---|---|---|---|---|---|---|---|---|
| Raw Score | Percentile Rank | Stanine | Raw Score | Percentile Rank | Stanine | Raw Score | Percentile Rank | Stanine |
| *** | *** | *** | *** | *** | *** | *** | *** | *** |
| *** | *** | *** | *** | *** | *** | *** | *** | *** |
| *** | *** | *** | *** | *** | *** | *** | *** | *** |
| 1 to 4 | 1 | 1 | *** | *** | *** | *** | *** | *** |
| 5 | 2 | 1 | *** | *** | *** | *** | *** | *** |
| 6 | 4 | 1 | *** | *** | *** | *** | *** | *** |
| 7 | 4 | 1 | *** | *** | *** | *** | *** | *** |
| 8 | 4 | 1 | 1 to 8 | 1 | 1 | *** | *** | *** |
| 9 | 6 | 2 | 9 | 2 | 1 | *** | *** | *** |
| 10 | 8 | 2 | 10 | 3 | 1 | *** | *** | *** |
| 11 | 12 | 3 | 11 | 3 | 1 | 1 to 11 | 1 | 1 |
| 12 | 17 | 3 | 12 | 5 | 2 | 12 | 3 | 1 |
| 13 | 20 | 3 | 13 | 6 | 2 | 13 | 4 | 1 |
| 14 | 23 | 3 | 14 | 9 | 2 | 14 | 5 | 2 |
| 15 | 27 | 4 | 15 | 12 | 3 | 15 | 8 | 2 |
| 16 | 31 | 4 | 16 | 15 | 3 | 16 | 10 | 2 |
| 17 | 35 | 4 | 17 | 18 | 3 | 17 | 13 | 3 |
| 18 | 39 | 4 | 18 | 22 | 3 | 18 | 15 | 3 |
| 19 | 43 | 5 | 19 | 27 | 4 | 19 | 17 | 3 |
| 20 | 46 | 5 | 20 | 31 | 4 | 20 | 20 | 3 |
| 21 | 48 | 5 | 21 | 34 | 4 | 21 | 21 | 3 |
| 22 | 51 | 5 | 22 | 36 | 4 | 22 | 23 | 3 |
| 23 | 56 | 5 | 23 | 39 | 4 | 23 | 27 | 4 |
| 24 | 60 | 5 | 24 | 43 | 5 | 24 | 30 | 4 |
| 25 | 64 | 6 | 25 | 44 | 5 | 25 | 32 | 4 |
| 26 | 67 | 6 | 26 | 45 | 5 | 26 | 36 | 4 |
| 27 | 70 | 6 | 27 | 49 | 5 | 27 | 41 | 5 |
| 28 | 73 | 6 | 28 | 55 | 5 | 28 | 45 | 5 |
| 29 | 76 | 6 | 29 | 58 | 5 | 29 | 49 | 5 |
| 30 | 78 | 7 | 30 | 61 | 6 | 30 | 53 | 5 |
| 31 | 82 | 7 | 31 | 66 | 6 | 31 | 55 | 5 |
| 32 | 85 | 7 | 32 | 72 | 6 | 32 | 60 | 5 |
| 33 | 87 | 7 | 33 | 78 | 7 | 33 | 64 | 6 |
| 34 | 89 | 7 | 34 | 81 | 7 | 34 | 68 | 6 |
| 35 | 91 | 8 | 35 | 81 | 7 | 35 | 72 | 6 |
| 36 | 94 | 8 | 36 | 85 | 7 | 36 | 76 | 6 |
| 37 | 97 | 9 | 37 | 89 | 7 | 37 | 81 | 7 |
| 38 | 98 | 9 | 38 | 92 | 8 | 38 | 85 | 7 |
| 39 to 44 | 99 | 9 | 39 | 94 | 8 | 39 | 88 | 7 |
| *** | *** | *** | 40 | 96 | 8 | 40 | 92 | 8 |
| *** | *** | *** | 41 | 96 | 8 | 41 | 95 | 8 |
| *** | *** | *** | 42 | 97 | 9 | 42 | 96 | 8 |
| *** | *** | *** | 43 | 98 | 9 | 43 | 98 | 9 |
| *** | *** | *** | 44 | 99 | 9 | 44 | 99 | 9 |
| *** | *** | *** | *** | *** | *** | *** | *** | *** |
| *** | *** | *** | *** | *** | *** | *** | *** | *** |
| *** | *** | *** | *** | *** | *** | *** | *** | *** |
| *** | *** | *** | *** | *** | *** | *** | *** | *** |
| *** | *** | *** | *** | *** | *** | *** | *** | *** |
| *** | *** | *** | *** | *** | *** | *** | *** | *** |

# Percentile Ranks and Stanines: ACCURACY    FORM 2

| Age 6:00 – 6:11 | | | Age 7:00 – 7:11 | | | Age 8:00 – 8:11 | | |
|---|---|---|---|---|---|---|---|---|
| Raw Score | Percentile Rank | Stanine | Raw Score | Percentile Rank | Stanine | Raw Score | Percentile Rank | Stanine |
| 1 | 1 | 1 | *** | *** | *** | *** | *** | *** |
| 2 | 2 | 1 | *** | *** | *** | *** | *** | *** |
| 3 | 3 | 1 | 1 to 3 | 1 | 1 | *** | *** | *** |
| 4 | 5 | 2 | 4 | 2 | 1 | *** | *** | *** |
| 5 | 6 | 2 | 5 | 3 | 1 | *** | *** | *** |
| 6 | 10 | 2 | 6 | 4 | 1 | *** | *** | *** |
| 7 | 15 | 3 | 7 | 5 | 2 | *** | *** | *** |
| 8 | 18 | 3 | 8 | 6 | 2 | *** | *** | *** |
| 9 | 19 | 3 | 9 | 7 | 2 | *** | *** | *** |
| 10 | 19 | 3 | 10 | 8 | 2 | *** | *** | *** |
| 11 | 21 | 3 | 11 | 9 | 2 | 1 to 11 | 1 | 1 |
| 12 | 24 | 4 | 12 | 11 | 2 | 12 | 2 | 1 |
| 13 | 28 | 4 | 13 | 13 | 3 | 13 | 3 | 1 |
| 14 | 32 | 4 | 14 | 17 | 3 | 14 | 4 | 1 |
| 15 | 35 | 4 | 15 | 20 | 3 | 15 | 5 | 2 |
| 16 | 38 | 4 | 16 | 22 | 3 | 16 | 5 | 2 |
| 17 | 41 | 5 | 17 | 23 | 3 | 17 | 7 | 2 |
| 18 | 44 | 5 | 18 | 24 | 4 | 18 | 8 | 2 |
| 19 | 47 | 5 | 19 | 25 | 4 | 19 | 9 | 2 |
| 20 | 47 | 5 | 20 | 28 | 4 | 20 | 10 | 2 |
| 21 | 48 | 5 | 21 | 31 | 4 | 21 | 11 | 2 |
| 22 | 50 | 5 | 22 | 32 | 4 | 22 | 13 | 3 |
| 23 | 52 | 5 | 23 | 35 | 4 | 23 | 14 | 3 |
| 24 | 53 | 5 | 24 | 38 | 4 | 24 | 15 | 3 |
| 25 | 54 | 5 | 25 | 39 | 4 | 25 | 17 | 3 |
| 26 | 57 | 5 | 26 | 41 | 5 | 26 | 17 | 3 |
| 27 | 61 | 6 | 27 | 42 | 5 | 27 | 19 | 3 |
| 28 | 64 | 6 | 28 | 43 | 5 | 28 | 21 | 3 |
| 29 | 66 | 6 | 29 | 44 | 5 | 29 | 22 | 3 |
| 30 | 67 | 6 | 30 | 45 | 5 | 30 | 24 | 4 |
| 31 | 69 | 6 | 31 | 47 | 5 | 31 | 26 | 4 |
| 32 | 72 | 6 | 32 | 49 | 5 | 32 | 27 | 4 |
| 33 | 73 | 6 | 33 | 51 | 5 | 33 | 28 | 4 |
| 34 | 74 | 6 | 34 | 52 | 5 | 34 | 29 | 4 |
| 35 | 75 | 6 | 35 | 54 | 5 | 35 | 29 | 4 |
| 36 | 76 | 6 | 36 | 55 | 5 | 36 | 30 | 4 |
| 37 | 78 | 7 | 37 | 57 | 5 | 37 | 31 | 4 |
| 38 | 79 | 7 | 38 | 60 | 5 | 38 | 33 | 4 |
| 39 | 80 | 7 | 39 | 61 | 6 | 39 | 34 | 4 |
| 40 | 82 | 7 | 40 | 62 | 6 | 40 | 36 | 4 |
| 41 | 83 | 7 | 41 | 65 | 6 | 41 | 38 | 4 |
| 42 | 85 | 7 | 42 | 68 | 6 | 42 | 40 | 4 |
| 43 | 86 | 7 | 43 | 70 | 6 | 43 | 43 | 5 |
| 44 | 86 | 7 | 44 | 71 | 6 | 44 | 47 | 5 |
| 45 | 87 | 7 | 45 | 72 | 6 | 45 | 50 | 5 |
| 46 | 88 | 7 | 46 | 73 | 6 | 46 | 52 | 5 |
| 47 | 90 | 8 | 47 | 76 | 6 | 47 | 53 | 5 |
| 48 | 92 | 8 | 48 | 79 | 7 | 48 | 54 | 5 |
| 49 | 92 | 8 | 49 | 81 | 7 | 49 | 56 | 5 |
| 50 | 92 | 8 | 50 | 83 | 7 | 50 | 59 | 5 |

continued on next page

# Percentile Ranks and Stanines: ACCURACY

FORM 2

| Age 6:00 – 6:11 | | | Age 7:00 – 7:11 | | | Age 8:00 – 8:11 | | |
|---|---|---|---|---|---|---|---|---|
| Raw Score | Percentile Rank | Stanine | Raw Score | Percentile Rank | Stanine | Raw Score | Percentile Rank | Stanine |
| 51 | 92 | 8 | 51 | 84 | 7 | 51 | 61 | 6 |
| 52 | 92 | 8 | 52 | 85 | 7 | 52 | 62 | 6 |
| 53 | 92 | 8 | 53 | 85 | 7 | 53 | 63 | 6 |
| 54 | 92 | 8 | 54 | 86 | 7 | 54 | 64 | 6 |
| 55 | 94 | 8 | 55 | 87 | 7 | 55 | 66 | 6 |
| 56 | 95 | 8 | 56 | 88 | 7 | 56 | 68 | 6 |
| 57 | 96 | 8 | 57 | 88 | 7 | 57 | 69 | 6 |
| 58 | 97 | 9 | 58 | 88 | 7 | 58 | 69 | 6 |
| 59 | 97 | 9 | 59 | 89 | 7 | 59 | 70 | 6 |
| 60 | 97 | 9 | 60 | 91 | 8 | 60 | 71 | 6 |
| 61 | 97 | 9 | 61 | 92 | 8 | 61 | 71 | 6 |
| 62 | 97 | 9 | 62 | 93 | 8 | 62 | 72 | 6 |
| 63 | 97 | 9 | 63 | 94 | 8 | 63 | 72 | 6 |
| 64 | 97 | 9 | 64 | 94 | 8 | 64 | 74 | 6 |
| 65 | 97 | 9 | 65 | 94 | 8 | 65 | 77 | 6 |
| 66 | 98 | 9 | 66 | 94 | 8 | 66 | 79 | 7 |
| 67 to 100 | 99 | 9 | 67 | 94 | 8 | 67 | 79 | 7 |
| *** | *** | *** | 68 | 94 | 8 | 68 | 81 | 7 |
| *** | *** | *** | 69 | 94 | 8 | 69 | 82 | 7 |
| *** | *** | *** | 70 | 94 | 8 | 70 | 83 | 7 |
| *** | *** | *** | 71 | 94 | 8 | 71 | 83 | 7 |
| *** | *** | *** | 72 | 94 | 8 | 72 | 83 | 7 |
| *** | *** | *** | 73 | 94 | 8 | 73 | 84 | 7 |
| *** | *** | *** | 74 | 94 | 8 | 74 | 85 | 7 |
| *** | *** | *** | 75 | 94 | 8 | 75 | 85 | 7 |
| *** | *** | *** | 76 | 95 | 8 | 76 | 85 | 7 |
| *** | *** | *** | 77 | 96 | 8 | 77 | 85 | 7 |
| *** | *** | *** | 78 | 96 | 8 | 78 | 86 | 7 |
| *** | *** | *** | 79 | 97 | 9 | 79 | 86 | 7 |
| *** | *** | *** | 80 | 98 | 9 | 80 | 87 | 7 |
| *** | *** | *** | 81 | 98 | 9 | 81 | 88 | 7 |
| *** | *** | *** | 82 | 98 | 9 | 82 | 90 | 8 |
| *** | *** | *** | 83 | 98 | 9 | 83 | 90 | 8 |
| *** | *** | *** | 84 | 98 | 9 | 84 | 92 | 8 |
| *** | *** | *** | 85 | 98 | 9 | 85 | 94 | 8 |
| *** | *** | *** | 86 | 98 | 9 | 86 | 95 | 8 |
| *** | *** | *** | 87 | 98 | 9 | 87 | 96 | 8 |
| *** | *** | *** | 88 | 98 | 9 | 88 | 96 | 8 |
| *** | *** | *** | 89 | 98 | 9 | 89 | 96 | 8 |
| *** | *** | *** | 90 | 98 | 9 | 90 | 96 | 8 |
| *** | *** | *** | 91 | 98 | 9 | 91 | 96 | 8 |
| *** | *** | *** | 92 | 98 | 9 | 92 | 97 | 9 |
| *** | *** | *** | 93 to 100 | 99 | 9 | 93 | 98 | 9 |
| *** | *** | *** | *** | *** | *** | 94 | 98 | 9 |
| *** | *** | *** | *** | *** | *** | 95 | 98 | 9 |
| *** | *** | *** | *** | *** | *** | 96 | 99 | 9 |
| *** | *** | *** | *** | *** | *** | 97 | 99 | 9 |
| *** | *** | *** | *** | *** | *** | 98 | 99 | 9 |
| *** | *** | *** | *** | *** | *** | 99 | 99 | 9 |
| *** | *** | *** | *** | *** | *** | 100 | 99 | 9 |

# Percentile Ranks and Stanines: ACCURACY

FORM 2

| Age 9:00 – 9:11 | | | Age 10:00 – 10:11 | | | Age 11:00 – 11:11 | | |
|---|---|---|---|---|---|---|---|---|
| Raw Score | Percentile Rank | Stanine | Raw Score | Percentile Rank | Stanine | Raw Score | Percentile Rank | Stanine |
| * * * | * * * | * * * | * * * | * * * | * * * | * * * | * * * | * * * |
| * * * | * * * | * * * | * * * | * * * | * * * | * * * | * * * | * * * |
| * * * | * * * | * * * | * * * | * * * | * * * | * * * | * * * | * * * |
| 1 to 14 | 1 | 1 | * * * | * * * | * * * | * * * | * * * | * * * |
| 15 | 2 | 1 | 1 to 15 | 1 | 1 | * * * | * * * | * * * |
| 16 | 3 | 1 | 16 | 2 | 1 | * * * | * * * | * * * |
| 17 | 3 | 1 | 17 | 2 | 1 | * * * | * * * | * * * |
| 18 | 3 | 1 | 18 | 2 | 1 | * * * | * * * | * * * |
| 19 | 3 | 1 | 19 | 2 | 1 | * * * | * * * | * * * |
| 20 | 3 | 1 | 20 | 2 | 1 | * * * | * * * | * * * |
| 21 | 3 | 1 | 21 | 2 | 1 | * * * | * * * | * * * |
| 22 | 3 | 1 | 22 | 3 | 1 | * * * | * * * | * * * |
| 23 | 3 | 1 | 23 | 3 | 1 | * * * | * * * | * * * |
| 24 | 3 | 1 | 24 | 3 | 1 | 1 to 24 | 1 | 1 |
| 25 | 4 | 1 | 25 | 3 | 1 | 25 | 2 | 1 |
| 26 | 5 | 2 | 26 | 4 | 1 | 26 | 2 | 1 |
| 27 | 5 | 2 | 27 | 4 | 1 | 27 | 2 | 1 |
| 28 | 6 | 2 | 28 | 4 | 1 | 28 | 2 | 1 |
| 29 | 8 | 2 | 29 | 4 | 1 | 29 | 2 | 1 |
| 30 | 9 | 2 | 30 | 4 | 1 | 30 | 3 | 1 |
| 31 | 9 | 2 | 31 | 5 | 2 | 31 | 3 | 1 |
| 32 | 11 | 2 | 32 | 5 | 2 | 32 | 3 | 1 |
| 33 | 13 | 3 | 33 | 5 | 2 | 33 | 3 | 1 |
| 34 | 13 | 3 | 34 | 5 | 2 | 34 | 3 | 1 |
| 35 | 14 | 3 | 35 | 5 | 2 | 35 | 3 | 1 |
| 36 | 14 | 3 | 36 | 6 | 2 | 36 | 4 | 1 |
| 37 | 15 | 3 | 37 | 7 | 2 | 37 | 5 | 2 |
| 38 | 17 | 3 | 38 | 7 | 2 | 38 | 5 | 2 |
| 39 | 19 | 3 | 39 | 7 | 2 | 39 | 6 | 2 |
| 40 | 20 | 3 | 40 | 8 | 2 | 40 | 6 | 2 |
| 41 | 22 | 3 | 41 | 8 | 2 | 41 | 7 | 2 |
| 42 | 24 | 4 | 42 | 10 | 2 | 42 | 8 | 2 |
| 43 | 26 | 4 | 43 | 12 | 3 | 43 | 9 | 2 |
| 44 | 27 | 4 | 44 | 13 | 3 | 44 | 9 | 2 |
| 45 | 28 | 4 | 45 | 13 | 3 | 45 | 11 | 2 |
| 46 | 29 | 4 | 46 | 14 | 3 | 46 | 12 | 3 |
| 47 | 31 | 4 | 47 | 16 | 3 | 47 | 12 | 3 |
| 48 | 33 | 4 | 48 | 17 | 3 | 48 | 12 | 3 |
| 49 | 34 | 4 | 49 | 19 | 3 | 49 | 13 | 3 |
| 50 | 35 | 4 | 50 | 19 | 3 | 50 | 15 | 3 |
| 51 | 38 | 4 | 51 | 20 | 3 | 51 | 15 | 3 |
| 52 | 39 | 4 | 52 | 21 | 3 | 52 | 16 | 3 |
| 53 | 42 | 5 | 53 | 23 | 3 | 53 | 18 | 3 |
| 54 | 45 | 5 | 54 | 23 | 3 | 54 | 20 | 3 |
| 55 | 46 | 5 | 55 | 25 | 4 | 55 | 21 | 3 |
| 56 | 49 | 5 | 56 | 29 | 4 | 56 | 21 | 3 |
| 57 | 51 | 5 | 57 | 32 | 4 | 57 | 23 | 3 |
| 58 | 52 | 5 | 58 | 32 | 4 | 58 | 25 | 4 |
| 59 | 53 | 5 | 59 | 33 | 4 | 59 | 26 | 4 |
| 60 | 53 | 5 | 60 | 34 | 4 | 60 | 27 | 4 |

continued on next page

# Percentile Ranks and Stanines: ACCURACY

FORM 2

| Age 9:00 – 9:11 | | | Age 10:00 – 10:11 | | | Age 11:00 – 11:11 | | |
|---|---|---|---|---|---|---|---|---|
| Raw Score | Percentile Rank | Stanine | Raw Score | Percentile Rank | Stanine | Raw Score | Percentile Rank | Stanine |
| 61 | 54 | 5 | 61 | 35 | 4 | 61 | 28 | 4 |
| 62 | 55 | 5 | 62 | 36 | 4 | 62 | 28 | 4 |
| 63 | 57 | 5 | 63 | 38 | 4 | 63 | 29 | 4 |
| 64 | 59 | 5 | 64 | 41 | 5 | 64 | 29 | 4 |
| 65 | 60 | 5 | 65 | 42 | 5 | 65 | 29 | 4 |
| 66 | 62 | 6 | 66 | 43 | 5 | 66 | 29 | 4 |
| 67 | 64 | 6 | 67 | 44 | 5 | 67 | 31 | 4 |
| 68 | 66 | 6 | 68 | 45 | 5 | 68 | 33 | 4 |
| 69 | 67 | 6 | 69 | 45 | 5 | 69 | 35 | 4 |
| 70 | 68 | 6 | 70 | 46 | 5 | 70 | 36 | 4 |
| 71 | 69 | 6 | 71 | 48 | 5 | 71 | 37 | 4 |
| 72 | 69 | 6 | 72 | 50 | 5 | 72 | 37 | 4 |
| 73 | 71 | 6 | 73 | 52 | 5 | 73 | 39 | 4 |
| 74 | 73 | 6 | 74 | 54 | 5 | 74 | 40 | 4 |
| 75 | 74 | 6 | 75 | 55 | 5 | 75 | 42 | 5 |
| 76 | 75 | 6 | 76 | 56 | 5 | 76 | 43 | 5 |
| 77 | 77 | 6 | 77 | 58 | 5 | 77 | 45 | 5 |
| 78 | 79 | 7 | 78 | 60 | 5 | 78 | 47 | 5 |
| 79 | 80 | 7 | 79 | 61 | 6 | 79 | 49 | 5 |
| 80 | 81 | 7 | 80 | 63 | 6 | 80 | 51 | 5 |
| 81 | 81 | 7 | 81 | 64 | 6 | 81 | 54 | 5 |
| 82 | 81 | 7 | 82 | 65 | 6 | 82 | 58 | 5 |
| 83 | 81 | 7 | 83 | 67 | 6 | 83 | 59 | 5 |
| 84 | 83 | 7 | 84 | 69 | 6 | 84 | 61 | 6 |
| 85 | 85 | 7 | 85 | 72 | 6 | 85 | 63 | 6 |
| 86 | 86 | 7 | 86 | 73 | 6 | 86 | 65 | 6 |
| 87 | 87 | 7 | 87 | 75 | 6 | 87 | 67 | 6 |
| 88 | 89 | 7 | 88 | 77 | 6 | 88 | 71 | 6 |
| 89 | 91 | 8 | 89 | 81 | 7 | 89 | 74 | 6 |
| 90 | 93 | 8 | 90 | 85 | 7 | 90 | 75 | 6 |
| 91 | 94 | 8 | 91 | 87 | 7 | 91 | 77 | 6 |
| 92 | 95 | 8 | 92 | 90 | 8 | 92 | 79 | 7 |
| 93 | 97 | 9 | 93 | 92 | 8 | 93 | 80 | 7 |
| 94 | 98 | 9 | 94 | 93 | 8 | 94 | 83 | 7 |
| 95 | 99 | 9 | 95 | 94 | 8 | 95 | 85 | 7 |
| 96 | 99 | 9 | 96 | 94 | 8 | 96 | 87 | 7 |
| 97 | 99 | 9 | 97 | 96 | 8 | 97 | 91 | 8 |
| 98 | 99 | 9 | 98 | 99 | 9 | 98 | 95 | 8 |
| 99 | 99 | 9 | 99 | 99 | 9 | 99 | 96 | 8 |
| 100 | 99 | 9 | 100 | 99 | 9 | 100 | 98 | 9 |

# Percentile Ranks and Stanines: RATE

FORM 2

| Age 6:00 – 6:11 | | | Age 7:00 – 7:11 | | | Age 8:00 – 8:11 | | |
|---|---|---|---|---|---|---|---|---|
| Raw Score | Percentile Rank | Stanine | Raw Score | Percentile Rank | Stanine | Raw Score | Percentile Rank | Stanine |
| *** | *** | *** | *** | *** | *** | *** | *** | *** |
| *** | *** | *** | *** | *** | *** | *** | *** | *** |
| *** | *** | *** | *** | *** | *** | *** | *** | *** |
| *** | *** | *** | *** | *** | *** | *** | *** | *** |
| *** | *** | *** | *** | *** | *** | *** | *** | *** |
| *** | *** | *** | *** | *** | *** | *** | *** | *** |
| *** | *** | *** | *** | *** | *** | *** | *** | *** |
| 1 to 8 | 1 | 1 | *** | *** | *** | *** | *** | *** |
| 9 | 2 | 1 | *** | *** | *** | *** | *** | *** |
| 10 | 4 | 1 | *** | *** | *** | 1 to 10 | 1 | 1 |
| 11 | 5 | 2 | 1 to 11 | 1 | 1 | 11 | 2 | 1 |
| 12 | 6 | 2 | 12 | 2 | 1 | 12 | 2 | 1 |
| 13 | 8 | 2 | 13 | 4 | 1 | 13 | 2 | 1 |
| 14 | 11 | 2 | 14 | 6 | 2 | 14 | 2 | 1 |
| 15 | 12 | 3 | 15 | 7 | 2 | 15 | 2 | 1 |
| 16 | 13 | 3 | 16 | 8 | 2 | 16 | 2 | 1 |
| 17 | 17 | 3 | 17 | 9 | 2 | 17 | 2 | 1 |
| 18 | 22 | 3 | 18 | 10 | 2 | 18 | 3 | 1 |
| 19 | 26 | 4 | 19 | 12 | 3 | 19 | 4 | 1 |
| 20 | 28 | 4 | 20 | 13 | 3 | 20 | 4 | 1 |
| 21 | 31 | 4 | 21 | 14 | 3 | 21 | 5 | 2 |
| 22 | 31 | 4 | 22 | 15 | 3 | 22 | 8 | 2 |
| 23 | 33 | 4 | 23 | 17 | 3 | 23 | 9 | 2 |
| 24 | 35 | 4 | 24 | 17 | 3 | 24 | 9 | 2 |
| 25 | 35 | 4 | 25 | 18 | 3 | 25 | 11 | 2 |
| 26 | 36 | 4 | 26 | 21 | 3 | 26 | 12 | 3 |
| 27 | 36 | 4 | 27 | 23 | 3 | 27 | 12 | 3 |
| 28 | 36 | 4 | 28 | 24 | 4 | 28 | 13 | 3 |
| 29 | 38 | 4 | 29 | 26 | 4 | 29 | 15 | 3 |
| 30 | 39 | 4 | 30 | 29 | 4 | 30 | 15 | 3 |
| 31 | 40 | 4 | 31 | 31 | 4 | 31 | 17 | 3 |
| 32 | 42 | 5 | 32 | 33 | 4 | 32 | 19 | 3 |
| 33 | 44 | 5 | 33 | 33 | 4 | 33 | 20 | 3 |
| 34 | 47 | 5 | 34 | 34 | 4 | 34 | 21 | 3 |
| 35 | 49 | 5 | 35 | 35 | 4 | 35 | 23 | 3 |
| 36 | 50 | 5 | 36 | 37 | 4 | 36 | 25 | 4 |
| 37 | 51 | 5 | 37 | 40 | 4 | 37 | 26 | 4 |
| 38 | 53 | 5 | 38 | 43 | 5 | 38 | 28 | 4 |
| 39 | 53 | 5 | 39 | 44 | 5 | 39 | 30 | 4 |
| 40 | 55 | 5 | 40 | 45 | 5 | 40 | 31 | 4 |
| 41 | 56 | 5 | 41 | 47 | 5 | 41 | 32 | 4 |
| 42 | 56 | 5 | 42 | 49 | 5 | 42 | 35 | 4 |
| 43 | 60 | 5 | 43 | 51 | 5 | 43 | 38 | 4 |
| 44 | 63 | 6 | 44 | 53 | 5 | 44 | 39 | 4 |
| 45 | 66 | 6 | 45 | 55 | 5 | 45 | 40 | 4 |
| 46 | 69 | 6 | 46 | 56 | 5 | 46 | 42 | 5 |
| 47 | 70 | 6 | 47 | 56 | 5 | 47 | 44 | 5 |
| 48 | 71 | 6 | 48 | 58 | 5 | 48 | 45 | 5 |
| 49 | 72 | 6 | 49 | 59 | 5 | 49 | 45 | 5 |
| 50 | 72 | 6 | 50 | 61 | 6 | 50 | 46 | 5 |

continued on next page

# Percentile Ranks and Stanines: RATE

FORM 2

| Age 6:00 – 6:11 | | | Age 7:00 – 7:11 | | | Age 8:00 – 8:11 | | |
|---|---|---|---|---|---|---|---|---|
| Raw Score | Percentile Rank | Stanine | Raw Score | Percentile Rank | Stanine | Raw Score | Percentile Rank | Stanine |
| 51 | 72 | 6 | 51 | 62 | 6 | 51 | 47 | 5 |
| 52 | 72 | 6 | 52 | 63 | 6 | 52 | 48 | 5 |
| 53 | 72 | 6 | 53 | 64 | 6 | 53 | 48 | 5 |
| 54 | 73 | 6 | 54 | 66 | 6 | 54 | 48 | 5 |
| 55 | 74 | 6 | 55 | 67 | 6 | 55 | 50 | 5 |
| 56 | 74 | 6 | 56 | 68 | 6 | 56 | 51 | 5 |
| 57 | 76 | 6 | 57 | 69 | 6 | 57 | 52 | 5 |
| 58 | 77 | 6 | 58 | 70 | 6 | 58 | 52 | 5 |
| 59 | 78 | 7 | 59 | 72 | 6 | 59 | 53 | 5 |
| 60 | 78 | 7 | 60 | 73 | 6 | 60 | 54 | 5 |
| 61 | 78 | 7 | 61 | 75 | 6 | 61 | 56 | 5 |
| 62 | 78 | 7 | 62 | 77 | 6 | 62 | 57 | 5 |
| 63 | 79 | 7 | 63 | 78 | 7 | 63 | 60 | 5 |
| 64 | 81 | 7 | 64 | 78 | 7 | 64 | 62 | 6 |
| 65 | 82 | 7 | 65 | 79 | 7 | 65 | 64 | 6 |
| 66 | 82 | 7 | 66 | 80 | 7 | 66 | 65 | 6 |
| 67 | 82 | 7 | 67 | 81 | 7 | 67 | 67 | 6 |
| 68 | 83 | 7 | 68 | 82 | 7 | 68 | 67 | 6 |
| 69 | 85 | 7 | 69 | 82 | 7 | 69 | 67 | 6 |
| 70 | 87 | 7 | 70 | 82 | 7 | 70 | 67 | 6 |
| 71 | 88 | 7 | 71 | 83 | 7 | 71 | 67 | 6 |
| 72 | 89 | 7 | 72 | 84 | 7 | 72 | 68 | 6 |
| 73 | 89 | 7 | 73 | 85 | 7 | 73 | 69 | 6 |
| 74 | 89 | 7 | 74 | 85 | 7 | 74 | 70 | 6 |
| 75 | 89 | 7 | 75 | 85 | 7 | 75 | 71 | 6 |
| 76 | 90 | 8 | 76 | 85 | 7 | 76 | 72 | 6 |
| 77 | 92 | 8 | 77 | 87 | 7 | 77 | 73 | 6 |
| 78 | 94 | 8 | 78 | 89 | 7 | 78 | 73 | 6 |
| 79 | 94 | 8 | 79 | 90 | 8 | 79 | 75 | 6 |
| 80 | 94 | 8 | 80 | 91 | 8 | 80 | 76 | 6 |
| 81 | 94 | 8 | 81 | 91 | 8 | 81 | 77 | 6 |
| 82 | 95 | 8 | 82 | 92 | 8 | 82 | 77 | 6 |
| 83 | 96 | 8 | 83 | 93 | 8 | 83 | 77 | 6 |
| 84 | 96 | 8 | 84 | 93 | 8 | 84 | 78 | 7 |
| 85 | 96 | 8 | 85 | 93 | 8 | 85 | 79 | 7 |
| 86 | 96 | 8 | 86 | 95 | 8 | 86 | 79 | 7 |
| 87 | 96 | 8 | 87 | 96 | 8 | 87 | 81 | 7 |
| 88 | 96 | 8 | 88 | 96 | 8 | 88 | 83 | 7 |
| 89 | 97 | 9 | 89 | 96 | 8 | 89 | 84 | 7 |
| 90 | 98 | 9 | 90 | 96 | 8 | 90 | 85 | 7 |
| 91 + | 99 | 9 | 91 | 97 | 9 | 91 | 85 | 7 |
| *** | *** | *** | 92 | 97 | 9 | 92 | 87 | 7 |
| *** | *** | *** | 93 | 97 | 9 | 93 | 88 | 7 |
| *** | *** | *** | 94 | 97 | 9 | 94 | 88 | 7 |
| *** | *** | *** | 95 | 97 | 9 | 95 | 88 | 7 |
| *** | *** | *** | 96 | 97 | 9 | 96 | 89 | 7 |
| *** | *** | *** | 97 | 98 | 9 | 97 | 89 | 7 |
| *** | *** | *** | 98 + | 99 | 9 | 98 | 90 | 8 |
| *** | *** | *** | *** | *** | *** | 99 | 91 | 8 |
| *** | *** | *** | *** | *** | *** | 100 | 92 | 8 |

continued on next page

## Percentile Ranks and Stanines: RATE

| Raw Score | Percentile Rank | Stanine | Raw Score | Percentile Rank | Stanine | Raw Score | Percentile Rank | Stanine |
|---|---|---|---|---|---|---|---|---|
| | | | | | | | | |
| *** | *** | *** | *** | *** | *** | 101 | 92 | 8 |
| *** | *** | *** | *** | *** | *** | 102 | 92 | 8 |
| *** | *** | *** | *** | *** | *** | 103 | 92 | 8 |
| *** | *** | *** | *** | *** | *** | 104 | 92 | 8 |
| *** | *** | *** | *** | *** | *** | 105 | 92 | 8 |
| *** | *** | *** | *** | *** | *** | 106 | 92 | 8 |
| *** | *** | *** | *** | *** | *** | 107 | 93 | 8 |
| *** | *** | *** | *** | *** | *** | 108 | 94 | 8 |
| *** | *** | *** | *** | *** | *** | 109 | 95 | 8 |
| *** | *** | *** | *** | *** | *** | 110 | 95 | 8 |
| *** | *** | *** | *** | *** | *** | 111 | 95 | 8 |
| *** | *** | *** | *** | *** | *** | 112 | 96 | 8 |
| *** | *** | *** | *** | *** | *** | 113 | 96 | 8 |
| *** | *** | *** | *** | *** | *** | 114 | 97 | 9 |
| *** | *** | *** | *** | *** | *** | 115 | 98 | 9 |
| *** | *** | *** | *** | *** | *** | 116 | 98 | 9 |
| *** | *** | *** | *** | *** | *** | 117 | 98 | 9 |
| *** | *** | *** | *** | *** | *** | 118 | 98 | 9 |
| *** | *** | *** | *** | *** | *** | 119 + | 99 | 9 |
| *** | *** | *** | *** | *** | *** | *** | *** | *** |

Column headers span three age groups: **Age 6:00 – 6:11**, **Age 7:00 – 7:11**, **Age 8:00 – 8:11**

# Percentile Ranks and Stanines: RATE

FORM 2

| Age 9:00 – 9:11 | | | Age 10:00 – 10:11 | | | Age 11:00 – 11:11 | | |
|---|---|---|---|---|---|---|---|---|
| Raw Score | Percentile Rank | Stanine | Raw Score | Percentile Rank | Stanine | Raw Score | Percentile Rank | Stanine |
| *** | *** | *** | *** | *** | *** | *** | *** | *** |
| *** | *** | *** | *** | *** | *** | *** | *** | *** |
| *** | *** | *** | *** | *** | *** | *** | *** | *** |
| *** | *** | *** | *** | *** | *** | *** | *** | *** |
| *** | *** | *** | *** | *** | *** | *** | *** | *** |
| *** | *** | *** | *** | *** | *** | *** | *** | *** |
| *** | *** | *** | *** | *** | *** | *** | *** | *** |
| *** | *** | *** | *** | *** | *** | *** | *** | *** |
| 1 to 20 | 2 | 1 | *** | *** | *** | *** | *** | *** |
| 21 | 2 | 1 | *** | *** | *** | *** | *** | *** |
| 22 | 2 | 1 | *** | *** | *** | *** | *** | *** |
| 23 | 2 | 1 | *** | *** | *** | *** | *** | *** |
| 24 | 2 | 1 | 1 to 24 | 1 | 1 | *** | *** | *** |
| 25 | 2 | 1 | 25 | 1 | 1 | *** | *** | *** |
| 26 | 2 | 1 | 26 | 2 | 1 | *** | *** | *** |
| 27 | 2 | 1 | 27 | 2 | 1 | *** | *** | *** |
| 28 | 2 | 1 | 28 | 2 | 1 | *** | *** | *** |
| 29 | 3 | 1 | 29 | 3 | 1 | *** | *** | *** |
| 30 | 4 | 1 | 30 | 3 | 1 | *** | *** | *** |
| 31 | 4 | 1 | 31 | 4 | 1 | *** | *** | *** |
| 32 | 4 | 1 | 32 | 4 | 1 | *** | *** | *** |
| 33 | 4 | 1 | 33 | 5 | 2 | 1 to 33 | 1 | 1 |
| 34 | 4 | 1 | 34 | 5 | 2 | 34 | 2 | 1 |
| 35 | 4 | 1 | 35 | 6 | 2 | 35 | 3 | 1 |
| 36 | 5 | 2 | 36 | 7 | 2 | 36 | 3 | 1 |
| 37 | 5 | 2 | 37 | 7 | 2 | 37 | 3 | 1 |
| 38 | 6 | 2 | 38 | 7 | 2 | 38 | 3 | 1 |
| 39 | 7 | 2 | 39 | 7 | 2 | 39 | 3 | 1 |
| 40 | 9 | 2 | 40 | 7 | 2 | 40 | 4 | 1 |
| 41 | 10 | 2 | 41 | 7 | 2 | 41 | 5 | 2 |
| 42 | 11 | 2 | 42 | 8 | 2 | 42 | 5 | 2 |
| 43 | 12 | 3 | 43 | 9 | 2 | 43 | 6 | 2 |
| 44 | 14 | 3 | 44 | 10 | 2 | 44 | 8 | 2 |
| 45 | 16 | 3 | 45 | 11 | 2 | 45 | 8 | 2 |
| 46 | 18 | 3 | 46 | 11 | 2 | 46 | 9 | 2 |
| 47 | 20 | 3 | 47 | 12 | 3 | 47 | 10 | 2 |
| 48 | 21 | 3 | 48 | 12 | 3 | 48 | 10 | 2 |
| 49 | 23 | 3 | 49 | 12 | 3 | 49 | 11 | 2 |
| 50 | 23 | 3 | 50 | 13 | 3 | 50 | 11 | 2 |
| 51 | 24 | 4 | 51 | 14 | 3 | 51 | 12 | 3 |
| 52 | 25 | 4 | 52 | 15 | 3 | 52 | 12 | 3 |
| 53 | 28 | 4 | 53 | 16 | 3 | 53 | 12 | 3 |
| 54 | 30 | 4 | 54 | 17 | 3 | 54 | 13 | 3 |
| 55 | 30 | 4 | 55 | 18 | 3 | 55 | 13 | 3 |
| 56 | 31 | 4 | 56 | 19 | 3 | 56 | 13 | 3 |
| 57 | 32 | 4 | 57 | 19 | 3 | 57 | 13 | 3 |
| 58 | 35 | 4 | 58 | 20 | 3 | 58 | 13 | 3 |
| 59 | 38 | 4 | 59 | 20 | 3 | 59 | 13 | 3 |
| 60 | 38 | 4 | 60 | 21 | 3 | 60 | 14 | 3 |

continued on next page

# Percentile Ranks and Stanines: RATE

FORM 2

| Age 9:00 – 9:11 | | | Age 10:00 – 10:11 | | | Age 11:00 – 11:11 | | |
|---|---|---|---|---|---|---|---|---|
| Raw Score | Percentile Rank | Stanine | Raw Score | Percentile Rank | Stanine | Raw Score | Percentile Rank | Stanine |
| 61 | 40 | 4 | 61 | 22 | 3 | 61 | 16 | 3 |
| 62 | 42 | 5 | 62 | 23 | 3 | 62 | 18 | 3 |
| 63 | 42 | 5 | 63 | 23 | 3 | 63 | 19 | 3 |
| 64 | 42 | 5 | 64 | 24 | 4 | 64 | 20 | 3 |
| 65 | 44 | 5 | 65 | 25 | 4 | 65 | 22 | 3 |
| 66 | 47 | 5 | 66 | 27 | 4 | 66 | 24 | 4 |
| 67 | 49 | 5 | 67 | 29 | 4 | 67 | 26 | 4 |
| 68 | 49 | 5 | 68 | 30 | 4 | 68 | 26 | 4 |
| 69 | 50 | 5 | 69 | 32 | 4 | 69 | 26 | 4 |
| 70 | 51 | 5 | 70 | 34 | 4 | 70 | 27 | 4 |
| 71 | 53 | 5 | 71 | 36 | 4 | 71 | 28 | 4 |
| 72 | 54 | 5 | 72 | 38 | 4 | 72 | 30 | 4 |
| 73 | 56 | 5 | 73 | 39 | 4 | 73 | 31 | 4 |
| 74 | 57 | 5 | 74 | 41 | 5 | 74 | 33 | 4 |
| 75 | 59 | 5 | 75 | 42 | 5 | 75 | 34 | 4 |
| 76 | 61 | 6 | 76 | 43 | 5 | 76 | 35 | 4 |
| 77 | 63 | 6 | 77 | 44 | 5 | 77 | 36 | 4 |
| 78 | 63 | 6 | 78 | 46 | 5 | 78 | 38 | 4 |
| 79 | 66 | 6 | 79 | 47 | 5 | 79 | 39 | 4 |
| 80 | 68 | 6 | 80 | 48 | 5 | 80 | 40 | 4 |
| 81 | 69 | 6 | 81 | 49 | 5 | 81 | 40 | 4 |
| 82 | 71 | 6 | 82 | 50 | 5 | 82 | 40 | 4 |
| 83 | 71 | 6 | 83 | 52 | 5 | 83 | 42 | 5 |
| 84 | 71 | 6 | 84 | 53 | 5 | 84 | 45 | 5 |
| 85 | 72 | 6 | 85 | 54 | 5 | 85 | 46 | 5 |
| 86 | 73 | 6 | 86 | 56 | 5 | 86 | 46 | 5 |
| 87 | 74 | 6 | 87 | 58 | 5 | 87 | 47 | 5 |
| 88 | 76 | 6 | 88 | 59 | 5 | 88 | 47 | 5 |
| 89 | 78 | 7 | 89 | 60 | 5 | 89 | 49 | 5 |
| 90 | 79 | 7 | 90 | 61 | 6 | 90 | 50 | 5 |
| 91 | 79 | 7 | 91 | 62 | 6 | 91 | 51 | 5 |
| 92 | 79 | 7 | 92 | 64 | 6 | 92 | 53 | 5 |
| 93 | 80 | 7 | 93 | 65 | 6 | 93 | 55 | 5 |
| 94 | 80 | 7 | 94 | 66 | 6 | 94 | 56 | 5 |
| 95 | 80 | 7 | 95 | 67 | 6 | 95 | 57 | 5 |
| 96 | 80 | 7 | 96 | 70 | 6 | 96 | 57 | 5 |
| 97 | 80 | 7 | 97 | 72 | 6 | 97 | 58 | 5 |
| 98 | 81 | 7 | 98 | 75 | 6 | 98 | 59 | 5 |
| 99 | 82 | 7 | 99 | 78 | 7 | 99 | 59 | 5 |
| 100 | 83 | 7 | 100 | 79 | 7 | 100 | 59 | 5 |
| 101 | 83 | 7 | 101 | 80 | 7 | 101 | 60 | 5 |
| 102 | 84 | 7 | 102 | 80 | 7 | 102 | 60 | 5 |
| 103 | 85 | 7 | 103 | 81 | 7 | 103 | 60 | 5 |
| 104 | 85 | 7 | 104 | 82 | 7 | 104 | 61 | 6 |
| 105 | 85 | 7 | 105 | 84 | 7 | 105 | 61 | 6 |
| 106 | 86 | 7 | 106 | 84 | 7 | 106 | 62 | 6 |
| 107 | 86 | 7 | 107 | 86 | 7 | 107 | 63 | 6 |
| 108 | 86 | 7 | 108 | 88 | 7 | 108 | 63 | 6 |
| 109 | 86 | 7 | 109 | 89 | 7 | 109 | 63 | 6 |
| 110 | 86 | 7 | 110 | 90 | 8 | 110 | 63 | 6 |

continued on next page

# Percentile Ranks and Stanines: RATE

FORM 2

| Age 9:00 – 9:11 | | | Age 10:00 – 10:11 | | | Age 11:00 – 11:11 | | |
|---|---|---|---|---|---|---|---|---|
| Raw Score | Percentile Rank | Stanine | Raw Score | Percentile Rank | Stanine | Raw Score | Percentile Rank | Stanine |
| 111 | 86 | 7 | 111 | 90 | 8 | 111 | 63 | 6 |
| 112 | 86 | 7 | 112 | 91 | 8 | 112 | 64 | 6 |
| 113 | 87 | 7 | 113 | 91 | 8 | 113 | 65 | 6 |
| 114 | 87 | 7 | 114 | 92 | 8 | 114 | 67 | 6 |
| 115 | 88 | 7 | 115 | 93 | 8 | 115 | 68 | 6 |
| 116 | 88 | 7 | 116 | 94 | 8 | 116 | 69 | 6 |
| 117 | 89 | 7 | 117 | 95 | 8 | 117 | 70 | 6 |
| 118 | 89 | 7 | 118 | 95 | 8 | 118 | 70 | 6 |
| 119 | 90 | 8 | 119 | 95 | 8 | 119 | 71 | 6 |
| 120 | 90 | 8 | 120 | 96 | 8 | 120 | 73 | 6 |
| 121 | 90 | 8 | 121 | 96 | 8 | 121 | 75 | 6 |
| 122 | 91 | 8 | 122 | 96 | 8 | 122 | 75 | 6 |
| 123 | 93 | 8 | 123 | 97 | 9 | 123 | 76 | 6 |
| 124 | 94 | 8 | 124 | 98 | 9 | 124 | 77 | 6 |
| 125 | 94 | 8 | 125 | 98 | 9 | 125 | 78 | 7 |
| 126 | 94 | 8 | 126 | 98 | 9 | 126 | 78 | 7 |
| 127 | 94 | 8 | 127 | 98 | 9 | 127 | 79 | 7 |
| 128 | 95 | 8 | 128 | 98 | 9 | 128 | 80 | 7 |
| 129 | 96 | 8 | 129 | 98 | 9 | 129 | 80 | 7 |
| 130 | 96 | 8 | 130 | 98 | 9 | 130 | 81 | 7 |
| 131 | 96 | 8 | 131 | 98 | 9 | 131 | 82 | 7 |
| 132 | 96 | 8 | 132 | 98 | 9 | 132 | 83 | 7 |
| 133 | 97 | 9 | 133 | 98 | 9 | 133 | 85 | 7 |
| 134 | 97 | 9 | 134 | 98 | 9 | 134 | 87 | 7 |
| 135 | 98 | 9 | 135 | 98 | 9 | 135 | 88 | 7 |
| 136 | 98 | 9 | 136 | 98 | 9 | 136 | 88 | 7 |
| 137 | 98 | 9 | 137 | 98 | 9 | 137 | 89 | 7 |
| 138 + | 99 | 9 | 138 + | 99 | 9 | 138 | 90 | 8 |
| *** | *** | *** | *** | *** | *** | 139 | 91 | 8 |
| *** | *** | *** | *** | *** | *** | 140 | 92 | 8 |
| *** | *** | *** | *** | *** | *** | 141 | 93 | 8 |
| *** | *** | *** | *** | *** | *** | 142 | 93 | 8 |
| *** | *** | *** | *** | *** | *** | 143 | 94 | 8 |
| *** | *** | *** | *** | *** | *** | 144 | 95 | 8 |
| *** | *** | *** | *** | *** | *** | 145 | 95 | 8 |
| *** | *** | *** | *** | *** | *** | 146 | 95 | 8 |
| *** | *** | *** | *** | *** | *** | 147 | 96 | 8 |
| *** | *** | *** | *** | *** | *** | 148 | 96 | 8 |
| *** | *** | *** | *** | *** | *** | 149 | 96 | 8 |
| *** | *** | *** | *** | *** | *** | 150 | 96 | 8 |
| *** | *** | *** | *** | *** | *** | 151 | 96 | 8 |
| *** | *** | *** | *** | *** | *** | 152 | 96 | 8 |
| *** | *** | *** | *** | *** | *** | 153 | 97 | 9 |
| *** | *** | *** | *** | *** | *** | 154 | 97 | 9 |
| *** | *** | *** | *** | *** | *** | 155 | 97 | 9 |
| *** | *** | *** | *** | *** | *** | 156 | 97 | 9 |
| *** | *** | *** | *** | *** | *** | 157 | 97 | 9 |
| *** | *** | *** | *** | *** | *** | 158 | 98 | 9 |
| *** | *** | *** | *** | *** | *** | 159 | 99 | 9 |
| *** | *** | *** | *** | *** | *** | 160 + | 99 | 9 |

# Percentile Ranks and Stanines: COMPREHENSION    FORM 2

| Age 6:00 – 6:11 | | | Age 7:00 – 7:11 | | | Age 8:00 – 8:11 | | |
|---|---|---|---|---|---|---|---|---|
| Raw Score | Percentile Rank | Stanine | Raw Score | Percentile Rank | Stanine | Raw Score | Percentile Rank | Stanine |
| 1 | 5 | 2 | 1 | 1 | 1 | 1 | 1 | 1 |
| 2 | 12 | 3 | 2 | 5 | 2 | 2 | 2 | 1 |
| 3 | 16 | 3 | 3 | 12 | 3 | 3 | 3 | 1 |
| 4 | 25 | 4 | 4 | 20 | 3 | 4 | 4 | 1 |
| 5 | 34 | 4 | 5 | 24 | 4 | 5 | 5 | 2 |
| 6 | 38 | 4 | 6 | 25 | 4 | 6 | 7 | 2 |
| 7 | 43 | 5 | 7 | 30 | 4 | 7 | 9 | 2 |
| 8 | 51 | 5 | 8 | 36 | 4 | 8 | 12 | 3 |
| 9 | 56 | 5 | 9 | 40 | 4 | 9 | 17 | 3 |
| 10 | 61 | 6 | 10 | 46 | 5 | 10 | 21 | 3 |
| 11 | 68 | 6 | 11 | 50 | 5 | 11 | 28 | 4 |
| 12 | 71 | 6 | 12 | 53 | 5 | 12 | 31 | 4 |
| 13 | 74 | 6 | 13 | 56 | 5 | 13 | 34 | 4 |
| 14 | 79 | 7 | 14 | 58 | 5 | 14 | 38 | 4 |
| 15 | 82 | 7 | 15 | 64 | 6 | 15 | 43 | 5 |
| 16 | 84 | 7 | 16 | 70 | 6 | 16 | 50 | 5 |
| 17 | 86 | 7 | 17 | 76 | 6 | 17 | 58 | 5 |
| 18 | 89 | 7 | 18 | 82 | 7 | 18 | 62 | 6 |
| 19 | 90 | 8 | 19 | 86 | 7 | 19 | 65 | 6 |
| 20 | 90 | 8 | 20 | 90 | 8 | 20 | 69 | 6 |
| 21 | 92 | 8 | 21 | 91 | 8 | 21 | 73 | 6 |
| 22 | 94 | 8 | 22 | 93 | 8 | 22 | 76 | 6 |
| 23 | 94 | 8 | 23 | 93 | 8 | 23 | 79 | 7 |
| 24 | 94 | 8 | 24 | 94 | 8 | 24 | 83 | 7 |
| 25 | 95 | 8 | 25 | 94 | 8 | 25 | 86 | 7 |
| 26 | 96 | 8 | 26 | 95 | 8 | 26 | 87 | 7 |
| 27 | 96 | 8 | 27 | 95 | 8 | 27 | 88 | 7 |
| 28 | 96 | 8 | 28 | 96 | 8 | 28 | 89 | 7 |
| 29 | 97 | 9 | 29 | 97 | 9 | 29 | 90 | 8 |
| 30 to 44 | 99 | 9 | 30 | 98 | 9 | 30 | 91 | 8 |
| *** | *** | *** | 31 | 98 | 9 | 31 | 93 | 8 |
| *** | *** | *** | 32 | 98 | 9 | 32 | 94 | 8 |
| *** | *** | *** | 33 | 98 | 9 | 33 | 95 | 8 |
| *** | *** | *** | 34 to 44 | 99 | 9 | 34 | 96 | 8 |
| *** | *** | *** | *** | *** | *** | 35 | 97 | 9 |
| *** | *** | *** | *** | *** | *** | 36 | 98 | 9 |
| *** | *** | *** | *** | *** | *** | 37 to 44 | 99 | 9 |
| *** | *** | *** | *** | *** | *** | *** | *** | *** |
| *** | *** | *** | *** | *** | *** | *** | *** | *** |
| *** | *** | *** | *** | *** | *** | *** | *** | *** |

# Percentile Ranks and Stanines: COMPREHENSION FORM 2

| Age 9:00 – 9:11 | | | Age 10:00 – 10:11 | | | Age 11:00 – 11:11 | | |
|---|---|---|---|---|---|---|---|---|
| Raw Score | Percentile Rank | Stanine | Raw Score | Percentile Rank | Stanine | Raw Score | Percentile Rank | Stanine |
| 1 | 1 | 1 | *** | *** | *** | *** | *** | *** |
| 2 | 1 | 1 | *** | *** | *** | *** | *** | *** |
| 3 | 2 | 1 | *** | *** | *** | *** | *** | *** |
| 4 | 2 | 1 | *** | *** | *** | *** | *** | *** |
| 5 | 2 | 1 | *** | *** | *** | *** | *** | *** |
| 6 | 3 | 1 | *** | *** | *** | *** | *** | *** |
| 7 | 5 | 2 | 1 to 7 | 1 | 1 | *** | *** | *** |
| 8 | 6 | 2 | 8 | 2 | 1 | *** | *** | *** |
| 9 | 7 | 2 | 9 | 3 | 1 | *** | *** | *** |
| 10 | 9 | 2 | 10 | 4 | 1 | *** | *** | *** |
| 11 | 12 | 3 | 11 | 5 | 2 | 1 to 11 | 1 | 1 |
| 12 | 13 | 3 | 12 | 6 | 2 | 12 | 2 | 1 |
| 13 | 15 | 3 | 13 | 9 | 2 | 13 | 3 | 1 |
| 14 | 19 | 3 | 14 | 11 | 2 | 14 | 7 | 2 |
| 15 | 22 | 3 | 15 | 14 | 3 | 15 | 9 | 2 |
| 16 | 26 | 4 | 16 | 18 | 3 | 16 | 11 | 2 |
| 17 | 34 | 4 | 17 | 22 | 3 | 17 | 14 | 3 |
| 18 | 40 | 4 | 18 | 27 | 4 | 18 | 16 | 3 |
| 19 | 43 | 5 | 19 | 30 | 4 | 19 | 19 | 3 |
| 20 | 45 | 5 | 20 | 33 | 4 | 20 | 21 | 3 |
| 21 | 48 | 5 | 21 | 38 | 4 | 21 | 24 | 4 |
| 22 | 51 | 5 | 22 | 42 | 5 | 22 | 27 | 4 |
| 23 | 56 | 5 | 23 | 47 | 5 | 23 | 30 | 4 |
| 24 | 63 | 6 | 24 | 50 | 5 | 24 | 36 | 4 |
| 25 | 68 | 6 | 25 | 53 | 5 | 25 | 42 | 5 |
| 26 | 72 | 6 | 26 | 58 | 5 | 26 | 45 | 5 |
| 27 | 76 | 6 | 27 | 62 | 6 | 27 | 48 | 5 |
| 28 | 80 | 7 | 28 | 66 | 6 | 28 | 50 | 5 |
| 29 | 81 | 7 | 29 | 68 | 6 | 29 | 54 | 5 |
| 30 | 82 | 7 | 30 | 71 | 6 | 30 | 59 | 5 |
| 31 | 84 | 7 | 31 | 75 | 6 | 31 | 63 | 6 |
| 32 | 87 | 7 | 32 | 80 | 7 | 32 | 65 | 6 |
| 33 | 90 | 8 | 33 | 85 | 7 | 33 | 69 | 6 |
| 34 | 93 | 8 | 34 | 88 | 7 | 34 | 75 | 6 |
| 35 | 96 | 8 | 35 | 90 | 8 | 35 | 81 | 7 |
| 36 | 98 | 9 | 36 | 92 | 8 | 36 | 86 | 7 |
| 37 to 44 | 99 | 9 | 37 | 94 | 8 | 37 | 92 | 8 |
| *** | *** | *** | 38 | 96 | 9 | 38 | 95 | 8 |
| *** | *** | *** | 39 | 98 | 9 | 39 | 96 | 8 |
| *** | *** | *** | 40 to 44 | 99 | 9 | 40 | 98 | 9 |
| *** | *** | *** | *** | *** | *** | 41 | 98 | 9 |
| *** | *** | *** | *** | *** | *** | 42 | 98 | 9 |
| *** | *** | *** | *** | *** | *** | 43 | 99 | 9 |
| *** | *** | *** | *** | *** | *** | 44 | 99 | 9 |
| *** | *** | *** | *** | *** | *** | *** | *** | *** |
| *** | *** | *** | *** | *** | *** | *** | *** | *** |
| *** | *** | *** | *** | *** | *** | *** | *** | *** |
| *** | *** | *** | *** | *** | *** | *** | *** | *** |
| *** | *** | *** | *** | *** | *** | *** | *** | *** |
| *** | *** | *** | *** | *** | *** | *** | *** | *** |

# References

ANASTASI, A. (1976). *Psychological testing*. New York: Macmillian.

ANDREWS, R.J., & ELKINS, J. (1971). The use of the Neale Analysis of Reading Ability with lower grade primary school children. *The Slow Learning Child*, **18**, 3-7.

BADCOCK, D., & LOVEGROVE, W. (1981). The effects of contrast, stimulus duration, and spatial frequency on visible persistence in normal and specifically disabled readers. *Journal of Experimental Psychology: Human Perception & Performance*, **7**, 495-505.

BODER, E. (1973). Developmental dyslexia: A diagnostic approach based on three atypical reading-spelling patterns. *Developmental Medicine and Child Neurology*, **15**, 663-687.

BRADLEY, L., & BRYANT, P. (1981). Visual memory and phonological skills in reading and spelling backwardness. *Psychological Research*, **43**, 198-199.

BRADLEY, L. & BRYANT, P. (1983). Categoriziing sounds and learning to read – A causal connection. *Nature*, **301** (5899), 419-421.

BRADLEY, L. & BRYANT, P. (1985). *Rhyme and reason in reading and spelling*. Ann Arbor: University of Michigan Press.

BRENNAN, M. (1979). *BRIM Manual: Brennan Record for the Interpretation of Miscues*. Wagga Wagga, NSW: Riverina College of Advanced Education.

BRUNER, J.S., & POSTMAN, L. (1949). Perception, cognition and behaviour. *Journal of Personality*, **18**, 14-31.

BRYANT, P., & BRADLEY, L. (1985). Phonetic analysis capacity and learning to read. *Nature*, **313**, 73-74.

BURKE, E. (1977). The probing of children's reading strategies. *Educational Studies*, **3**, 137-143.

BURROUGHS, G. (1957). *A study of the vocabulary of young children*. Edinburgh: Oliver & Boyd.

BUSHELL, R., MILLER, A., & ROBSON, D. (1982). Parents as remedial teachers: An account of a paired reading project with junior school failing readers and their parents. *AEP Journal*, **5** (9), 7-13.

CARROLL, J.B. (1964). *Language and thought*. Englewood Cliffs, N.J.: Prentice-Hall.

CARROLL, J.B., DAVIES, P., & RICHMAN, B. (1971). *Word frequency book*. New York: American Heritage Publishing Co.

CHADWICK, O., RUTTER, M., THOMSON, J., & SHAFFER, D. (1981). Intellectual performance and reading skills after localized head injury in childhood. *Journal of Child Psychology and Psychiatry and Allied Disciplines*, **22**, 117-139.

CHAMBERLAIN, R.N., CHRISTIE, P.N., HOLT, K.S., HUNTLEY, R.M.C., POLLARD, R., & ROCHE, M.C. (1983). A study of school children who had identified virus infections of the central nervous system during infancy. *Child Care, Health and Development*, **9**, 29-47.

CLARK, M.M. (1970). *Reading difficulties in schools*. Harmondsworth, Middlesex: Penguin Books.

CLAY, M.M. (1972). *Reading: The patterning of complex behaviour*. South Yarra, Vic.: Heinemann.

CLAY, M.M. (1979). *The early detection of reading difficulties: A diagnostic survey with recovery procedures* (2nd ed.) Auckland, N.Z.: Heinemann.

COLBOURN, M.J., & McLEOD, J. (1983). The potential and feasibility of computer-guided educational diagnosis. In R.E.A. Mason (Ed.) *Information processing 83: Proceedings of the IFIP 9th World Computer Congress* (pp. 891-896). Amsterdam: Elsevier Science.

COLTHEART, M., PATTERSON, K., & MARSHALL, J.C. (Eds.). (1980). *Deep dyslexia*, London: Routledge & Kegan Paul.

CROFT, C. (1983). Spell-Write: An Aid to Writing, Spelling and Word Study. Wellington: NZCER.

CROFT, C., GILMORE, A., REID, N., & JACKSON, P. (1981). *Proof-reading tests of spelling.* Wellington: NZCER.

CRONBACH, L.J. (1951)*Coefficient Alpha and the internal structure of tests.* Psychometrika **16**, 297-334.

DEPARTMENT OF EDUCATION AND SCIENCE. (1975). *A language for life* (Report of the Committee of Inquiry appointed by the Secretary of State for Education and Science under the Chairmanship of Sir Alan Bullock). London: HMSO.

DOLCH, E.W. (1951). *Psychology and teaching of reading.* Champaign, Illinois: The Gerrard Press.

DOWNING, J. (1965). *The initial teaching alphabet explained and illustrated.* London: Cassell.

DOWNING, J., & CHE KAN LEONG. (1982). *Psychology of reading.* New York: Macmillan.

DYSON, J., & SWINSON, J. (1982). Involving parents in the teaching of reading: An account of a parent participation project involving failing readers in a primary school. *AEP Journal,* **5** (9), 18-21.

ELLIS, N.C., & MILES, T.R. (1981). A lexical encoding deficiency: Experimental evidence. In G.R. Pavlidis & T.R. Miles (Eds.), *Dyslexia research: Its application to education* (pp. 177-215). London: John Wiley.

FERNALD, G.M. (1943). *Remedial techniques in basic school subjects.* New York: McGraw-Hill.

FERNANDEZ, J.A. (1975). *Doñana: Spain's wildlife wilderness.* London: Collins.

FORSTER, C. (1984). *Adelaide – A social atlas* (Atlas of population and housing, 1981 Census, Vol. 5). Canberra: AGPS.

FRITH, U. (Ed.). (1980). *Cognitive processes in spelling.* London: Academic Press.

GATES, A.I. (1947). *The improvement of reading.* New York: Macmillan.

GIBSON, E.J., & LEVIN, H. (1975). *The psychology of reading.* Cambridge, Massachusetts: MIT Press.

GIBSON, J.J., & GIBSON, E.J. (1955). Perceptual learning, differentiation or enrichment. *Psychological Review,* **62**, 32-41.

GILLINGHAM, A.M., & STILLMAN, B.H. (1956). *Remedial training for children with specific disability in reading, spelling and penmanship* (5th ed.). New York: Sackett & Wilhelms.

GILMORE, A., CROFT, C., & REID, N. (1981). *Burt word reading test: New Zealand revision.* Wellington: NZCER.

GOODACRE, E., WHITE, J., & BRENNAN, P. (1980). Whatever happened to the black cat? *Reading Education,* **5** (2), 41-49.

GOODMAN, K.S. (1968). The psycholinguistic nature of the reading process. In K.S. Goodman (Ed.), *The psycholinguistic nature of the reading process* (pp. 13-26). Detroit, Michigan: Wayne State University Press.

GOODMAN, Y.M., & BURKE, C.L. (1972). *Reading miscue inventory: Manual of procedure for diagnosis and evaluation.* New York. Macmillan.

GRONLUND, N.E. (1981). *Measurement and evaluation in teaching.* New York: Macmillan.

GUILFORD, J.P. (1965). *Fundamental statistics in psychology and education.* New York: McGraw-Hill.

HARDING, L.M., BEECH, J.R., & SNEDDON, W. (1985). The changing pattern of reading errors and reading style from 5 to 11 years of age. *British Journal of Educational Psychology,* **55**, 45-52.

HAY, D.A., O'BRIEN, P.J., JOHNSTON, C.J., & PRIOR, M. (1984). The high incidence of reading disability in twin boys and its implications for genetic analyses. *Acta Geneticae Medicae et Gemellologiae,* **33**, 223-236.

HORNSBY, B., & MILES, T.R. (1980). The effects of a dyslexia-centred teaching programme. *British Journal of Educational Psychology,* **50**, 236-242.

JOHNSON, B. (1979). *Reading appraisal guide.* Hawthorn, Vic.: ACER.

JOHNSTON, C., PRIOR, M., & HAY, D. (1984). Prediction of reading disability in twin boys. *Developmental Medicine and Child Neurology,* **26**, 588-595.

JORM, A.F. (1983). *The psychology of reading and spelling disabilities.* London: Routledge & Kegan Paul.

LE COULTRE, E., & CARROLL, M. (1981). The effect of visualizing speech rhythms on reading comprehension and fluency. *Journal of Reading Behaviour,* **13**, 279-285.

LIBERMAN, I.Y., MANN, V.A., SHANKWEILER, D., & WERFELMAN, D. (1982). Children's memory for recurring linguistic and non-linguistic material in relation to reading ability. *Cortex,* **18**, 367-375.

LINDAMOOD, C.H., & LINDAMOOD, P.C. (1969). *The A.D.D. Program: Auditory discrimination in depth.* Boston: Teaching Resources Corporation.

LORD, F.M. (1952). *A theory of test scores* (Psychometric Monograph No. 7). Chicago: University of Chicago Press.

LORIMER, J. (1977). *Manual of directions and norms: Neale Analysis of Reading Ability adapted for use with blind children.* Windsor, Berks.: NFER.

LOVEGROVE, W., HEDDLE, M., & SLAGHUIS, W. (1980). Reading disability: Spatial frequency specific deficits in visual information store. *Neuropsychologia,* **18**, 111-115.

LOVEGROVE, W., MARTIN, F., BOWLING, A., BLACKWOOD, M., BADCOCK, D., & PAXTON, S. (1982). Contrast sensitivity functions and specific reading disability. *Neuropsychologia,* **20**, 309-315.

LYMAN, H.B. (1978). *Test scores and what they mean.* Englewood Cliffs, N.J.: Prentice-Hall.

McKAY, M.F. (1977). *A four year longitudinal study of reading performance.* Unpublished Master of Education Thesis, Monash University.

MITCHELL, D.C. (1982). *The process of reading: A cognitive analysis of fluent reading and learning to read.* Chichester, N.Y.: Wiley.

MOORHOUSE, A.J., & YULE, W. (1974). A comparison of the Neale and the Daniels and Diack reading tests. *Reading,* **8** (3), 24-27.

NEALE, M.D. (1956). *The construction and standardization of a diagnostic reading test.* Unpublished Ph.D. thesis, University of Birmingham, U.K.

NEALE, M.D. (1958). *Neale analysis of reading ability manual.* London: Macmillan.

NEALE, M.D. (1976). Neale Scales of Early Childhood Development. Sydney: Science Research Associates.

NEALE, M.D. (1988) *Neale Analysis of Reading Ability – Revised. Manual.* Melbourne (Australian Council for Educational Research).

NEALE, M.D., & McKAY, M.F. (1985). A three year longitudinal study of academic performance related to pre-school developmental characteristics on the Neale Scales of Early Childhood Development. Unpublished paper, Monash University.

NEALE, M.D., McKAY, M.F., & CHILDS, G. (1986). The Neale Analysis of Reading Ability – Revised. *British Journal of Educational Psychology*, **56**, 346-356.

NEISSER, U. (1967). *Cognitive psychology*. New York: Appleton-Century-Crofts.

NETLEY, C., RACHMAN, S., & TURNER, R.K. (1965). The effects of practice on performance in a reading attainment test. *British Journal of Educational Psychology*, **35**, 1-8.

PETERS, M. (1975). *Diagnostic and remedial spelling manual*. Basingstoke, Hants: Macmillan.

PUMFREY, P.D. (1977). *Measuring reading abilities: Concepts, sources and applications*. London: Hodder & Stoughton Educational.

RIDING, R.J., & PUGH, J.C. (1977). Iconic memory and reading performance in nine-year-old children. *British Journal of Educational Psychology*, **47**, 132-137.

RIDING, R.J., & WILLETTS, D. (1980). The relationship between dark interval threshold, sex and reading performance in nine-year-old children. *Educational Studies*, **6**, 211-216.

RINSLAND, H.D. (1945). *A basic vocabulary of elementary school children*. Oklahoma City: University of Oklahoma Press.

RUTTER, M., CHADWICK, O., SHAFFER, D., & BROWN, G. (1980). A prospective study of children with head injuries: I. Design and methods. *Psychological Medicine*, **10**, 633-645.

RUTTER, M., TIZARD, J., & WHITMORE, K. (1970). *Education, health and behaviour*. New York: Wiley.

SALVIA, J., & YSSELDYKE, J.E. (1981). *Assessment in special and remedial education*. Boston: Houghton Mifflin.

SATZ, P. (1976). Cerebral dominance and reading disability: An old problem revisited. In R. Knights and D.J. Bakker (Eds.) *The neuropsychiatry of learning disorders: Theoretical approaches*. Baltimore: University Park Press.

SCHONELL, F.J. (1948). *The psychology and teaching of reading*. London: Oliver & Boyd.

SCHONELL, F.J. (1950). *Diagnostic and attainment testing*. London: Oliver & Boyd.

SCHONELL, F.J., & GOODACRE, E. (1974). *The psychology and teaching of reading* (5th ed.) Edinburgh: Oliver & Boyd.

SEMEL, E. (1970). *Sound, order, sense: A developmental program in auditory perception*. Chicago: Follett Publishing Co.

SMITH, F. (1978). *Understanding reading: A psycholinguistic analysis of reading and learning to read* (2nd ed.). New York: Holt, Rinehart & Winston.

SMITH, F., & GOODMAN, K.S. (1971). On the psycholinguistic method of teaching reading. *Elementary School Journal*, **71**, 177-181.

SMITH, F., GOODMAN, K.S., & MEREDITH, R. (1970). *Language and thinking in the elementary school*. London: Holt, Rinehart & Winston.

SOLOMON, R.L., & POSTMAN, L. (1951). Frequency of usage as a determinant of recognition thresholds for words. *Journal of Experimental Psychology*, **43**, 195-201.

STEDMAN, J.A., & VAN HEYNINGEN, R. (1982). Educational underachievement and epilepsy: A study of children from normal schools, admitted to a special hospital for epilepsy. *Early Child Development and Care*, **9**, 65-82,

STORES, G. (1978). School children with epilepsy at risk for learning and behavioural problems. *Developmental Medicine and Child Neurology*, **20**, 502-508.

STURGE, C. (1982). Reading retardation and anti-social behaviour. *Journal of Child Psychology and Psychiatry and Allied Disciplines,* **23**, 21-31.

TEW, B., & LAWRENCE, K.M. (1978). Differences in reading achievement between spina bifida children attending normal schools and those attending special schools. *Child Care, Health and Development,* **4**, 317-326.

THOMPSON, G.B. (1987). Three studies of predicted gender differences in processes of word reading. *Journal of Educational Research,* **80**, 212-219.

THOMSON, M.E. (1984). *Developmental dyslexia: Its nature, assessment and remediation.* London: Edward Arnold.

THORNDIKE, E.L., & LORGE, I. (1944). *The teacher's word book of 30,000 words.* New York: Bureau of Publications, Teachers' College, Columbia University.

THURSTONE, L.L. (1944). *A factorial study of perception* (Psychometric Monograph No. 4). Chicago: University of Chicago Press.

VERNON, M. (1977). Varieties of deficiency in the reading processes. *Harvard Educational Review,* **37**, 396-410.

VERNON, P.E. (1938). *The standardization of a graded word reading test.* London: London University Press.

VERNON, P.E. (1949). A preliminary investigation of the vocabulary of Scottish children entering school: Word counts of 'infant readers'. *Studies in Reading, Volume 1.* London: University of London Press.

VINCENT, D., & DE LA MARE, M. (1985). *New Macmillan reading analysis.* Basingstoke, Hants: Macmillan.

WECHSLER, D. (1974). *Manual for WISC-R – Wechsler Intelligence Scale for Children – Revised.* New York: The Psychological Corporation.

WEPMAN, J. (1968). *Auditory discrimination test.* Chicago: Language Research Associates.

YULE, W. (1967). Predicting reading ages on Neale's Analysis of Reading Ability. *British Journal of Educational Psychology,* **37**, 252-255.

YULE, W. (1973). Differential prognoses of reading backwardness and specific reading retardation. *British Journal of Educational Psychology,* **43**, 244-248.

YULE, W., BERGER, M., RUTTER, M., & YULE, B. (1975). Children of West Indian immigrants: II. Intellectual performance and reading attainment. *Journal of Child Psychology and Psychiatry and Allied Disciplines,* **16**, 1-17.

YULE, W., LANSDOWN, R., & URBANOWICZ, M. (1982). Predicting educational attainment from WISC-R in a primary school sample. *British Journal of Clinical Psychology,* **21**, 43-46.

# Glossary

**Accommodation.** A Piagetian concept by which the individual, in assimilating new experiences, adjusts to new levels of functioning.

**Accuracy Raw Score.** The sum of the scores for individual passages read up to the ceiling after points have been deducted for errors made (p. 17).

**Adaptation.** The process by which an interchange occurs between the individual and the environment, modifying the individual in such a way that subsequent interchanges are facilitated.

**Age-appropriate passage.** A term that refers to the passage designed as 'appropriate' in interest and difficulty level to a given age group; hence Passage One, age six years; Passage Two, age seven years, etc. (p. 42).

**Age differentiation.** An aspect of validity concerned with children performing progressively better on each aspect of the test as they grow older (p. 56).

**Analysis.** The term chosen to best describe the assessment process, favoured by Neale, when exploring and measuring the reading skills of an individual pupil.

**Assimilation.** A process by which elements in a milieu (environment) are incorporated into the system.

**Attainment test.** An achievement test that indicates how much an individual knows about a particular content area, e.g., maths or reading.

**Attention.** The process of selectively or preferentially focusing on or responding to a stimulus or range of stimuli; a prerequisite for perception, memory, and all types of learning activities (p. 28).

**Auditory blending/Auditory closure.** The ability of the listener to fill in missing parts of words or conversation that the listener has not heard completely because of foreign accents, speech defects, back-ground noise, etc. (p. 32).

**Auditory discrimination.** The ability of a listener to detect differences in the initial, middle, or end segments of pairs of words when presented orally (p. 28 and 32).

**Auditory perception.** The psychological ability to process or use information received through the hearing system.

**Auditory sequencing.** The ability to temporally order units of information (sounds, words, numbers, etc.) for further processing (p. 37).

**Basal level.** The point at which it is assumed that the individual would receive full credit for all easier (earlier) items in the test (pp. 11, 17 and 18).

**Blending.** The ability to identify the constituent components of a word (either phonemes or syllables) pronounced by another, and to merge them to reproduce the original word orally (p. 32).

**Ceiling.** The point at which it is assumed that the student would not be able to receive credit by further testing, i.e. the point at which the permissible number of errors has been reached (p. 12).

**'Cloze' exercises.** Exercises that require the reader (or writer) to fill in missing words, letters, or parts of sentences (pp. 24 and 38).

**Cognitive processing.** The various aspects of mental activity which are presumed to underlie outward behaviour. In the context of this test, where the outward behaviour is reading aloud, among the mental processes involved are: perception, short-term memory, long-term memory, letter recognition, word recognition and comprehension. It is thought that the cognitive processes involved in reading change as children become more experienced readers.

**Comprehension Questions.** These are the prescribed questions, following each passage, that the examiner puts orally to the individual being tested.

**Comprehension Raw Score.** This is the score for the total number of questions correctly answered on passages read with 16 or fewer errors (20 on passage 6).

**Concurrent validity.** The aspect of validity that is established by correlating a test score with some valued measure (or measures) other than the test itself (p. 52).

**Construct validity.** The extent to which a test may be said to measure a theoretical construct or trait. It is usually assessed by evaluating any data that might help explain the nature of the trait in question, e.g. age differentiation, correlations with other tests, factor analysis.

**Content validity.** The determination of whether the content of a test covers a representative sample of the behaviour domain to be measured (p. 52).

**Contextual cues.** Other non-verbal, grammatical, or semantic information that may assist the reader in deriving meaning from what is being read (p. 7).

**Contextual error.** An oral reading error assumed to be 'forced' by a misinterpretation of the context (meaning, syntax, etc.) of the passage.

**Conversion Tables.** The tables in the Manual that allow the user to convert raw scores for Rate, Accuracy, and Comprehension to standardized scores such as Reading Ages, Percentile Ranks, and Stanines.

**Creative synthesis.** The process by which the examinee reconstructs his or her own interpretation of what has been read (p. 37).

**Criterion-referenced test.** An informal assessment device that compares the individual's performance with an aspect of the curriculum rather than the performances of other children (p. 25).

**Criterion-related validity.** The extent to which performance on the test is related to some other valued measure of performance; can be concerned with predictive relationships or concurrent relationships.

**Deprivation.** The absence, loss or removal of something desired, loved, or needed for subsequent development to occur satisfactorily.

**Diagnostic teaching.** An approach to teaching that aims at matching the learner, the task, and instructional interventions in a manner that facilitates maximum cognitive and emotional growth.

**Diagnostic test.** A test that aims at establishing patterns of strength and weakness in an individual's responses to its items.

**Diagnostic Tutor Form.** A 'parallel' form of the Neale Analysis of Reading Ability-Revised that has been designed for the purpose of informal diagnosis (p. 23).

**Dyslexia.** An inability to process the written word notwithstanding adequate intelligence and instruction.

**Equivalent Age Range.** In this Manual, the modelled equivalent age range within which an individual's true score probably lies (p. 21).

**Errors.** The incorrect responses made by the individual when orally reading the prose passages (p. 14).

**Extension Passage.** The more difficult passage contained in the Diagnostic Tutor Form entitled 'Coto Doñana'.

**Factor analysis.** The mathematical process by means of which one finds the smallest number of factors (products that can be multiplied together) that can account for a correlational matrix (p. 57).

**Forms 1 and 2.** The two standardized parallel forms of the Neale Analysis of Reading Ability-Revised.

**Grammatical structure.** The major linguistic features of the passages including the phonology and morphology of the words, semantics, and syntax of the sentences.

**Grapho-phonic errors.** The incorrect responses made by the reader that reveal inadequate, inappropriate, or deficient use of phonic knowledge in decoding words (p. 26).

**Individual Records.** The colour-coded scoring sheets for recording both qualitative and quantitative performance as the individual reads from the Reader. Separate Individual Records are available for each of the standardized forms and the Diagnostic Tutor Form.

**Inferential comprehension.** The ability to understand implied meaning in what is written (p. 41).

**Informal appraisal.** Assessment without rigid administration, scoring, and interpretation rules; includes criterion-referenced tests, task analyses, inventories of skills, etc. (p. 24).

**Informal reading inventory.** An informal assessment procedure that most often measures word recognition and comprehension skills; analysis of outcomes indicates whether the material is at an instructional, independent, or frustrational level for the reader (p. 24).

**Information processing.** The term used to describe the system of taking in linguistic information, organizing it, and carrying out an appropriate response.

**Internal consistency reliability.** A measure of the internal agreement of the test items; the extent to which they measure the same function here expressed as a correlation coefficient derived from a formula by Cronbach called coefficient alpha.

**Interval threshold perception.** The amount of time it takes (usually expressed in hundredths of a second) for a person to detect a difference, change, etc. in two or more visual stimuli or events (p. 57).

**Item analysis.** The process of establishing the difficulty level of items and their ability to discriminate between children of differing abilities (or ages) (p. 42).

**Key for Comprehension questions.** Sets of acceptable answers to the Comprehension questions associated with each passage.

**Kinesthetic cues.** A term for sensations of the body, received through the proprioreceptors which produce an awareness of movement, position of the body, and muscle tone.

**Language experience.** An approach to the teaching of reading skills that aims at integrating such skills with those of listening, speaking, and writing.

**Literal comprehension.** A level of understanding of written text that requires little, if any, interpretation on the part of the reader.

**Longitudinal Studies.** Studies which follow the same individuals over a period of time. A feature of such studies is that individual performance at the outset may be compared with later performance.

**The Manual.** The book containing all information relevant to the administration, scoring, and standardization of the Neale Analysis of Reading Ability-Revised.

**Maturation.** Development, or the process of attaining maturity through the expression of the underlying genetic blue print for growth and species-specific behaviour.

**Mean ($\bar{x}$).** The arithmetic average of a set of values, e.g. test scores for a class: the sum of the scores divided by the number of students in the class.

**Miscue analysis.** A psycholinguistically based analysis of the kind of mistakes children make when they read (p. 25).

**Narrative.** One of the terms used in this Manual to describe the stories or passages contained in the Reader.

**Neurological dysfunction.** A disorder in one or more of the cerebral processes underlying language, sensory, or motor functions (p. 28).

**Neurophysiology.** The branch of physiology that deals with the function of the nervous system.

**Normative scores.** Scores pertaining to the norms or standards.

**Normative testing.** Testing that results in a comparison of a student's performance with that of the students in the norm group (p. 7).

**Norms.** Representative standards or values for a given group; may be expressed in terms of age averages, percentile ranks, stanines, etc.

**Parallel forms.** An alternative (equivalent) form of the same test; in this case, Forms 1 and 2. Parallel forms make it possible to avoid practice effects when retesting to assess improvement.

**Parallel forms reliability.** *See* Stability reliability.

**Passage.** *See* Narrative.

**Percentile rank.** A score that translates student test performance into the percentage of norm-group students that performed as well as, or poorer than, that student on the same test (p. 19).

**Perception.** The psychological ability to process or use information received through the sense organs.

**Phoneme-grapheme relationships.** The alphabetic, orthographic representation of phonemes. In English there are about forty phonemes (perhaps a few more) that serve to make up, in various combinations, the sound system of the language.

**Phonics.** A term often imprecisely used, the origin of which is in the word 'phonetic'. 'Phonics' has become a blanket term to encompass instruction in correspondence between written and spoken language (p. 28).

**Practice Passages.** The two introductory narratives in the Reader designed to be read before formal testing begins to orient the reader to the assessment process (p. 7).

**Predictive validity.** A form of criterion-related validity; it refers to the ability of the test to predict later reading performance accurately (p. 54).

**Prompts.** In the context of the Neale Analysis of Reading Ability – Revised, the term that refers to the words given to the reader by the test administrator to correct an error.

**Psycholinguistics.** The study of mental processes that underlie the acquisition and use of language.

**Qualitative observations.** Those observations about the reader that describe him or her more fully as a person; non-standardized observations of reading behaviour.

**Rapport.** The quality of communication in the relationship between the test administrator and the reader (p. 11).

**Raw Score.** The first test score calculated before conversion to a standard score; *see also* Accuracy Raw Score, Comprehension Raw Score, and Reading Rate Raw Score.

**Raw Score Summary.** The section on the front cover of the Individual Record where each Raw Score is tabulated and summarized (p. 18 and Individual Records).

**The Reader.** The book that accompanies this Manual, in which is contained the narratives or passages for the standardized Forms 1 and 2 and the Diagnostic Tutor Form. It also contains the materials needed to administer the Supplementary Diagnostic Tests.

**Reading Ages.** The scores for Rate, Accuracy, and Comprehension expressed as age-equivalent scores. Statistically they are the predicted chronological ages for a reader's obtained raw scores for Rate, Accuracy, and Comprehension (p. 21).

**Reading backwardness.** General delay in reading ability in comparison with age peers.

**Reading Rate Raw Score.** The average rate of words read per minute. This is calculated by dividing the total number of words read by the time taken to read them (in seconds) and multiplying that value by 60 (p. 18).

**Reliability.** Refers to the consistency of a test; types of reliability include test-retest, parallel forms, split-half, and internal consistency (p. 49).

**Sample.** Term used to describe the group that was chosen to be representative of the population for which the Neale Analysis was designed (p. 47).

**Semantic errors.** Incorrect responses in the child's oral reading that suggest inappropriate processing of meaning, concepts, or vocabulary in the written text (p. 26).

**Sensorimotor system.** The combined functioning of the sense modalities and motor mechanisms.

**Short-term memory.** Immediate recall of events, verbal or visual stimuli, etc. (p. 28).

**Sound discrimination.** The ability to detect differences between similar sounds, e.g. 't', 'b', 'p' (pp. 30 and 32).

**Sound-symbol relationships.** Term commonly used to describe spelling-to-sound correspondences and orthographic (spelling pattern) constraints (p. 28).

**Specific reading disability.** A term used to describe the condition of a small proportion of children who experience difficulties with reading, spelling, or writing notwithstanding good instruction and adequate intelligence.

**Spelling Test.** One of the Supplementary Diagnostic Tests of the Neale Analysis of Reading Ability – Revised. It tests the child's ability to spell simple words both in context and out of context (p. 31).

**Stability reliability.** The reliability associated with the likelihood of obtaining similar scores on the two standardized forms of the Neale Analysis of Reading Ability – Revised.

**Standard deviation (SD).** A statistic that represents the variability of scores about the mean for a given sample.

**Standard error of measurement.** A statistic that estimates the amount of measurement error in the obtained scores. In the case of the Neale Analysis – Revised, in 68 per cent of cases the reader's true score can be assumed to lie within the limits of the Age Range.

**Standardization.** The process by which scores were obtained that led to the establishment of norms for the Neale Analysis of Reading Ability – Revised (p. 47).

**Standardized test.** A test in which the administration, scoring, and interpretation procedures are standard or set and for which norms are usually provided.

**Stanines.** Derived scores that are equivalent to a range of standard scores; they divide the normal distribution into nine ranges (p. 20).

**Supplementary Diagnostic Tests.** The four extra tests supplied with the Neale Analysis of Reading Ability – Revised, to assess subskills of discrimination of initial and final sounds in spoken language, names and sounds of the alphabet, spelling, and auditory discrimination and blending (p. 30).

**Syntactic (syntax) errors.** The incorrect responses made by the reader that are assumed to be the result of incorrect processing of the syntax of the sentence (p. 26).

**Syntax.** The grammatical arrangement of words that forms the structure of a sentence.

**Test selection table.** A check list of objectives with associated or appropriate choices (p. 9).

**Themes.** The conceptual framework or main idea in each passage written for the Neale Analysis of Reading Ability-Revised (p. 40).

**Tutoring.** Used in this Manual in its broadest sense to denote the process of instruction and coaching engaged in by the teacher or specialist with the pupil after an assessment and analysis of the individual's reading skills (p. 36).

**Validity.** The degree to which a test measures what it sets out to measure; types of validity include content, criterion (predictive and concurrent), and construct (p. 52).

**Visual perception.** Recognition of a visual quality as a result of a complex set of reactions including sensory stimulation, organization within the nervous system, and memory.

**Visual sequencing.** The ability to retain visually presented items in memory in their original spatial order.